SARAH DALLAS **KNITTING**

SARAH DALLAS **KNITTING**

PHOTOGRAPHS **CATHERINE GRATWICKE**

ROWAN

To Georgie

First published in 2005 by
Rowan Yarns
Green Mill Lane
Holmfirth
West Yorkshire
HD9 2DX

Designed and Art Directed by **Georgina Rhodes** and **Richard Proctor**
Styled by **Francine Kay**
Edited by **Sally Harding**
Pattern writer **Eva Yates**
Pattern checker **Stella Smith**

British Library Cataloguing in Publication Data A catalogue record
of this book is available from the British Library

ISBN 1 904485 29 4
Printed in Singapore

Contents

Introduction

This book was inspired by a family holiday in Dorset several years ago, which reminded me of holidays I spent as a child playing on the beach and then wrapping up to go home at the end of the day. The changeable weather during an English summer necessitates being prepared for all eventualities, hence clothes for enjoying the afternoon sun, for protection against the wind and for keeping warm on cool evenings. Therefore, my designs for this book include sweaters, cardigans, jackets, socks, blankets, cushions and even a vest.

All are functional pieces: blankets to throw down on the beach to have a picnic and later to envelop yourself at night, socks to wear inside or outside, and cardigans and jackets for comfort and style.

The mood of the book, perhaps subconsciously, reflects my own lifestyle; living in London yet craving the calmer comforts of life in the country, memories of childhood, playing with friends outside, rambling across the fields or along the beach, collecting leaves, flowers and pebbles. The designs combine the feeling of a modern, urban life with traditional crafts; of contrasts coming together.

Colour is one of the most important elements for me in the design process. The changing colours of the seasons are particularly inspiring: the crisp, sharp flushes of spring, the intense, vivid hues of summer, the rich, warm glows of autumn and the dark, sombre shades of winter. The combinations, the proportions and the balance of colours, whether in large areas, stripes, Fair Isles or the fine detail of a colour-tipped edge of a blanket, cushion or cardigan, are all critical.

Flowers are a constant source of inspiration and provide the spectrum of colours chosen for the book. The clean fresh colours of tulips, lilac, cornflowers and lavender and the bright, vibrant hues of poppies, peonies, roses, gerberas and ranunculus, alongside the blacks and greys of the urban environment, create contrasting groupings of colour that eventually work together as a whole.

Shape and silhouette are also crucial to any design, as are the type and quality of yarn used: crisp cottons, soft wools, knobbly tweeds and slubby silks, and never more importantly so when the pieces have a simplicity to them for a modern, contemporary lifestyle.

The final outcome is a collection of easy, functional pieces to knit for the family, the home, the garden and the beach.

Sarah Dallas
London, January 2005

LAVENDER/ROSE

Late summer and early autumn have a richness in the colour palette that never fails to inspire me. From the last flush of brilliant flowers against a golden sky to the cosy warmth of evenings as they draw in, there is a magical element to the closing days of summer. Colder evenings ask for warm socks, blankets to cuddle up in, a cardigan to slip over a summer dress. Lavender, rose, crimson and lime combine in unexpected ways to give quite simple designs an unusual twist.

Cotton Cardigan
In vibrant pink double knit cotton, this cardigan with its neat ribbed collar and pocket details is the ideal cover-up for cooler evenings. Simple to knit, it has garter-stitch rib panels on the front and sleeves. Page 22.

Stripy Socks

Ideal for padding around the house on cool mornings or evenings, these crimson and fuchsia pink striped socks are knitted in cosy 4ply Soft. With the toes and heels picked out in red, and with a contrasting coloured tip to the ribs, they look as good as they feel. Page 24.

Fair Isle Socks

With their simple Fair Isle border, these socks are knitted in the same yarn as the stripy pair. Page 25.

Gloves

These gloves are also knitted in the same yarn as the socks, and are similarly tipped with a contrasting colour at the ribs. Page 26.

Rothko-style Blanket
Inspired by Mark Rothko's bold abstract paintings, this blanket could not be simpler. Knitted in three strong colours, with fine contrasting borders, it creates a marvellous splash of brilliant colour. Page 28.

Rothko-style Cushion
The cushion is designed to coordinate with the blanket (left), incorporating the same vivid blocks of colour divided by the sharpness of the lime. Page 29.

Beret

In flattering lavender
4ply Soft, this classic
beret suits everyone.
The contrasting tip to
the rib provides just the
right touch of colour.
Page 30.

Three-textured Blanket
Knitted in crisp cotton yarn, in blocks of three different garter-stitch patterns, this textured blanket is in shades of lilac and pink, offset with details of sharp lemon and lime.
Page 31.

Cotton Cardigan

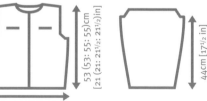

46 (49: 52: 55)cm
[18 (19½: 20½: 21½)in]

53 (53: 55: 55)cm
[21 (21: 21½: 21½)in]

44cm [17½ in]

SIZES & YARN

Size	S	M	L	XL	
To fit bust	86	91	96	102	cm
	34	36	38	40	in
Actual size	92	98	104	110	cm
	36	38½	41	43½	in
Back length	53	53	55	55	cm
	21	21	21½	21½	in
Sleeve seam	44	44	44	44	cm
	17½	17½	17½	17½	in

Rowan Handknit DK Cotton

Pink (313)	13	14	15	16	x 50g

9 buttons

NEEDLES

1 pair each of 3.25mm (US 3) and 4mm (US 6) needles. Stitch holder.

TENSION

20 sts and 28 rows to 10cm (4in) measured over st st using 4mm (US 6) needles.

BACK

Using 3.25mm (US 3) needles, cast on 86 (90: 98: 102) sts and work in garter rib as folls.

Row 1 *K2, P2, rep from * to last 2 sts, K2.
Row 2 P to end.
Rows 3 to 14 As rows 1 and 2, six times. Sizes 2 and 4 ONLY, inc 1 st at each end of last row. Change to 4mm (US 6) needles and st st, inc 1 st at each end of 13th and every foll 16th row to 92 (98: 104: 110) sts. Cont without shaping until work meas 32 (32: 33: 33)cm [12½ (12½: 13: 13)in], ending with RS facing for next row.

Shape armholes

Rows 1 and 2 Cast off 2 (3: 4: 4) sts, work to end.
Row 3 K2, sl1, K1, psso, knit to last 4 sts, K2tog, K2.
Row 4 P to end.
Rep rows 3 and 4 until 78 (82: 84: 88) sts rem. Cont without shaping until work meas 51 (51: 53: 53)cm [20 (20: 21: 21)in], ending with RS facing for next row.

Shape shoulders

Cast off 5 (5: 6: 6) sts at beg of next 6 rows. Cast off 6 (7: 5: 6) sts beg next 2 rows. Cast off.

POCKETS (make 2)

Using 4mm (US 6) needles, cast on 18 sts and work 28 rows in st st. Leave sts on holder.

LEFT FRONT

Using 3.25mm (US 3) needles, cast on 42 (44: 48: 50) sts and work 14 rows in garter rib as folls.

Row 1 *K2, P2, rep from * to last 2 (0: 0: 2) sts, K2 (0: 0: 2).
Row 2 P to end.
Rows 3 to 14 As rows 1 and 2, 6 times. Sizes 2 and 4 ONLY, inc 1 st at end of last row. Change to 4mm (US 6) needles and work as folls.
Row 1 K14 (19: 18: 23), *P2, K2, rep from * three times, P2, K10 (8: 12: 10).
Row 2 P to end.
Rows 1 and 2 form st st with garter rib panel patt. Cont in patt, inc 1 st at beg of 11th and every foll 16th row to 45 (48: 51: 54) sts. Cont without shaping until work meas 32 (32: 33: 33)cm [12½ (12½: 13: 13)in], ending with RS facing for next row.

Shape armhole

Row 1 (RS) Cast off 2 (3: 4: 4) sts, patt to end.
Row 2 P to end.
Row 3 K2, sl1, K1, psso, patt to end.
Row 4 P to end.

Rows 5 to 10 As rows 3 and 4, three times. 39 (41: 43: 46) sts.

Row 11 K2, sl1, K1, psso, K7 (11: 9: 14), *P2, K2, rep from *, cast off 2 sts, *K2, P2, rep from *, K10 (8: 12: 10).

Row 12 P18 (16: 20: 18), cast on 2 sts, P to end.

Rows 13 (K2, sl1, K1, psso) 0 (0: 1: 1) times, patt to end.

Row 14 P to end.

Row 15 (K2, sl1, K1, psso) 0 (0: 0: 1) times, patt to end.

Row 16 P10 (8: 12: 10), cast off 18 sts, P to end.

Row 17 K10 (14: 11: 15), K across pocket stitches, K to end. 38 (40: 41: 43) sts.

Row 18 P to end.

Cont in st st, without shaping, until work meas 48.5 (48.5: 50.5: 50.5)cm [19 (19: 20: 20)in], ending with **WS** facing for next row.

Shape neck

Cast off 8 (9: 9: 10) sts at beg of next row, knit to end. Dec 1 st at neck edge on next 6 rows.

Shape shoulders

Row 1 Cast off 5 (5: 6: 6) sts, K to last 2 sts, K2tog.

Row 2 P to end.

Rows 3 to 6 As rows 1 and 2, twice. Cast off.

RIGHT FRONT

Using 3.25mm (US 3) needles, cast on 42 (44: 48: 50) sts and work 14 rows in garter rib as folls.

Row 1 K2 (0: 0: 2), *P2, K2, rep from * to end.

Row 2 P to end.

Rows 3 to 14 As rows 1 and 2, six times. Sizes 2 and 4 ONLY, inc 1 st at beg of last row.
Change to 4mm (US 6) needles and patt as folls.

Row 1 K10 (8: 12: 10), *P2, K2, rep from * 3 times, P2, K to end.

Row 2 P to end.

This sets patt panel. Work to match left front, reversing all shaping.

SLEEVES (make 2)

Using 3.25mm (US 3) needles, cast on 46 (48: 50: 52) sts and work 14 rows in garter rib, noting **Row 1** K0 (1: 2: 3), *P2, K2, rep from * to last 2 (3: 0: 1) sts, P2 (2: 0: 0), K0 (1: 0: 1).
Change to 4mm (US 6) needles and cont as folls.

Row 1 K16 (17: 18: 19) *P2, K2, rep from * twice, P2, K16 (17: 18: 19).

Row 2 P to end.

These two rows form patt panel. Cont in patt, making fully fashioned incs by K2, inc, patt to

last 4 sts, inc, K3, on next and every foll 8th row to 74 (76: 78: 80) sts. Cont without shaping until work meas 44cm (17½in).

Shape sleevehead

Cast off 2 (3: 4: 4) sts at beg of next 2 rows.

Row 3 K2, sl1, K1, psso, patt to last 4 sts, K2tog, K2.

Row 4 P to end.

Rep rows 3 and 4 until 46 sts rem.
Dec 1 st at each end of next 4 rows. Cast off 3 sts at beg of next 4 rows. Cast off.

BUTTON BAND (Left front)

Using 3.25mm (US 3) needles, cast on 7 sts and work in K1, P1 rib until band, when slightly stretched, fits front from hem to neck. Cast off. Stitch into place. Mark positions for 7 buttonholes, the first 2 rows above the cast-on edge; the 2nd at top of garter rib; the 7th, 1cm (½in) below the neck; and the rem 4 evenly spaced between (approx 8cm [3in] apart).

BUTTONHOLE BAND (Right front)

Using 3.25mm (US 3) needles, cast on 7 sts. Working in K1, P1 rib, make buttonholes to match marked positions as folls.

Row 1 Rib 3, cast off 2 sts, rib to end.

Row 2 Rib 2, cast on 2 sts, rib to end.

Work to match button band length. Cast off. Stitch into place.

COLLAR

Using 4mm (US 6) needles, cast on 90 (90: 94: 98) sts and work as folls.

Row 1 *P2, K2, rep from * to last 2 sts, P2.

Row 2 P to end.

Rep rows 1 and 2 until work measures 8cm (3in), ending with row 1.

Next row P2 (2: 4: 6), *P2tog, P4, rep from * to last 4 (4: 6: 8) sts, P2tog, P2 (2: 4: 6). Cast off.

MAKING UP

Slipstitch pockets into position. Join shoulder and side seams. Join sleeve seams. Ease sleevehead into armhole and stitch into place. Place RS of collar to WS of garment, cast-off collar edge to neck, starting and finishing halfway across front bands. Oversew into place. Weave in any loose ends. Sew buttons on button band and on fronts to match buttonholes on pockets. Press lightly using a warm iron over a damp cloth.

Stripy Socks

SIZES & YARNS

To fit	S-M	M-L	
Foot length	24	26	cm
	9½	10	in

Rowan 4ply Soft

A Pink (377)	2	2	x 50g
B Red (374)	1	1	x 50g
C Light green (379)	1	1	x 50g

NEEDLES

4 x 3mm (US 2/3) double-ended needles.
4 x 3.75mm (US 5) double-ended needles.
Spare needle.

TENSION

26 sts and 32 rows to 10cm (4in) measured over st st using 3.75mm (US 5) needles.

SOCKS

Using 3mm (US 2/3) needles and yarn C, cast on 66 sts (22 sts on each of 3 needles). Break yarn C, join in yarn B and work 2.5cm (1in) in K1, P1 rib.
Change to 3.75mm (US 5) needles, join in yarn A and work as folls.

Rounds 1 to 6 Using yarn A, K to end.
Round 7 Using yarn B, K2, K2tog, K to last 4 sts, sl1, K1, psso, K2.
Round 8 Using yarn B, K to end.
Rounds 1 to 8 form stripe patt.
Rep rounds 1 to 8 until 52 sts rem. Cont in stripe patt without shaping until work meas approx 26cm (10in), ending on round 6. Break yarns.
Divide sts for heel Slip first 13 sts (on needle 1) and last 13 sts (on needle 3) onto spare needle. Arrange rem sts onto 2 needles for instep. Rejoin yarn B and work 20 rows in st st on heel sts, ending with RS facing for next row.
Row 21 K17, K2tog tbl, turn.
Row 22 Sl1, P8, P2tog, turn.
Row 23 Sl1, K8, K2tog tbl, turn.
Rep rows 22 and 23 until 10 sts rem.
Next row K10, pick up 10 sts from side of heel, with 2nd needle, K18 from instep sts, with 3rd needle K8, pick up 10 sts from side of heel (20: 18: 18 sts).
Work in rounds as folls.
K17, K2tog, K27, rearrange sts as folls: join in yarn A, K1, sl1, K1, psso, K16; needle 2, K18; needle 3, K18.

Round 1 K1, sl1, K1, psso, K22, K2tog, K to end.
Round 2 K to end.
Round 3 K1, sl1, K1, psso, K20, K2tog, K to end. 50 sts.
Knit 2 more rounds.
*Knit 2 rounds yarn B, 6 rounds yarn A, rep from * until foot measures 20 (22)cm [8 (8½)in]. Break yarn A.
Shape toe
Using yarn B, work as folls.
Round 1 and alt rounds K to end.
Round 2 *K1, sl1, K1, psso, K19, K2tog, K1, rep from *.
Round 4 *K1, sl1, K1, psso, K17, K2tog, K1, rep from *.
Round 6 *K1, sl1, K1, psso, K15, K2tog, K1, rep from *.
Rounds 7 to 12 Cont dec as set.
Round 13 K to end.
Cast off.
Make second sock to match.

MAKING UP

Oversew cast-off edge to make a flat seam. Weave in any loose ends. Press lightly using a warm iron over a damp cloth.

Fair Isle Socks

SIZES & YARNS

To fit	S-M	M-L	
Foot length	24	26	cm
	9	10	in

Rowan 4ply Soft

A Lavender (375)	2	2	x 50g
B Pink (377)	1	1	x 50g
C Light green (379)	1	1	x 50g
D Pale blue (370)	1	1	x 50g

NEEDLES

4 x 3mm (US 2/3) double-ended needles.
4 x 3.25mm (US 3) double-ended needles.
Spare needle.

TENSION

28 sts and 36 rows to 10cm (4in) measured
over st st using 3.25mm (US 3) needles.

SOCKS

Using 3mm (US 2/3) needles and yarn C, cast
on 64 sts (21: 21: 22 sts). Join in yarn B and
work 10 rounds in K1, P1 rib.
Change to 3.25mm (US 3) needles and work
Fair Isle in st st (every round, knit), joining in

yarns A and D, as folls.
Round 1 D.
Round 2 *2D, 3A, 3D, 2A, 3D, 2A, 1D, rep from
* to end.
Round 3 *1D, 5A, 3D, 2A, 1D, 2A, 2D, rep from *
to end.
Round 4 *2B, 3C, 3B, 3C, 1B, 3C, 1B, rep from *
to end.
Round 5 As round 3.
Round 6 As round 2.
Round 7 As round 1.
Break yarns C and D.
Change to stripe patt as folls.
Rounds 1 and 2 B.
Rounds 3 to 8 A.
Rounds 1 to 8 form stripe patt rep.
Rep rounds 1 to 8, three times.
Decrease round K2, K2tog, K to last 4 sts, sl1,
K1, psso, K2.
Cont in stripe pattern, dec as set on every foll
5th round until 48 sts rem.
Cont without shaping until work meas approx
33cm (13in), ending on round 8.
Break yarns.
Divide sts for heel Slip first 12 sts (on needle
1) and last 12 sts (on needle 3) onto spare

needle. Arrange rem sts onto 2 needles for
instep. Rejoin yarn B and work 20 rows in st st
on heel sts.
Row 21 K16, K2tog tbl, turn.
Row 22 Sl1, P8, P2tog, turn.
Row 23 Sl1, K8, K2tog tbl, turn.
Rep rows 22 and 23 until 10 sts rem.
Next row K10, pick up 10 sts from side of heel,
with 2nd needle, K16 from instep sts, with 3rd
needle K8, pick up 10 sts from side of heel
(20: 16: 18 sts).
Work in rounds as folls.
K17, K2tog, K25, rearrange sts as folls: join in
yarn A, K1, sl1, K1, psso, K16; needle 2, K16;
needle 3, K18.
Round 1 K1, sl1, K1, psso, K22, K2tog, K to end.
Round 2 K to end.
Round 3 K1, sl1, K1, psso, K20, K2tog, K to
end. 48 sts.
Knit 2 more rounds.
*Knit 2 rounds B, 6 rounds A, rep from * until
foot measures 20 (22)cm [8 (8½)in].
Break yarn A.
Shape toe
Using yarn B, work as folls.
Round 1 and alt rounds K to end.

Round 2 *K1, sl1, K1, psso, K18, K2tog, K1, rep
from *.
Round 4 *K1, sl1, K1, psso, K16, K2tog, K1, rep
from *.
Round 6 *K1, sl1, K1, psso, K14, K2tog, K1, rep
from *.
Rounds 7 to 12 Cont dec as set.
Round 13 K to end.
Cast off.
Make second sock to match.

MAKING UP

Oversew cast-off edge to make a flat seam.
Weave in any loose ends. Press lightly using a
warm iron over a damp cloth.

Gloves

SIZES & YARNS

Size	S-M	M-L	
Rowan 4ply Soft			
A Pink (377)	2	2	x 50g
B Light green (379)	Small amount for edging.		
C Lavender (375)	Small amount for edging.		

NEEDLES

4 x 2.75mm (US 2) double-ended needles.
Spare needles.
Safety pin.

TENSION

32 sts and 40 rows to 10cm (4in) measured
over st st using 2.75mm (US 2) needles.

RIGHT GLOVE

Using 2.75mm (US 2) needles and yarn B, cast
on 60 sts (20 sts on each of 3 needles). Break
yarn B.
Join in yarn A and work 6cm (2½in) in rounds
of K1, P1 rib. Change to st st (every round, knit)
and work 2 rounds.
Shape thumb gusset
Round 3 K30, inc, K2, inc, K to end.
Knit 3 rounds.
Round 7 K30, inc, K4, inc, K to end.
Knit 3 rounds.
Round 11 K30, inc, K6, inc, K to end.
Cont inc as set to completion of round 23.
72 sts.
Knit 2 rounds.
Round 26 K29, place next 18 sts on safety pin
for thumb, cast on 6 sts, complete the round.
60 sts.
Work 20 rounds.
Divide for fingers Slip first 22 sts of round onto
spare needle and rejoin yarn A with RS facing.
First finger
**K18 as folls, using spare needle 1, K6, using
spare needle 2, K10, turn, cast on 2 sts, turn.
Divide the 18 sts on spare needle onto 3
needles and knit 24 (30) rounds.
Shape top
Round 1 (K2tog) 9 times.
Round 2 K to end.
Round 3 *K1, K2tog, rep from * to end.
Break yarn, leaving an end to run through the
sts, pull up tightly and fasten off.
Second finger
RS facing, rejoin yarn A and K8, cast on 2 sts,
knit the last 8 sts of the rem sts, then pick up
and knit 2 sts from the base of the first finger.
Divide these 20 sts onto 3 needles and knit 28
(34) rounds.
Shape top
Round 1 *K2tog, rep from * to end.
Round 2 K to end.
Round 3 *K2tog, rep from * to end.
Break yarn, leaving an end to run through the
sts, pull up tightly and fasten off.
Third finger
RS facing, rejoin yarn A and K7, cast on 2 sts,
knit the last 7 sts of the rem sts, then pick up
and knit 2 sts from the base of the second
finger. Divide these 18 sts onto 3 needles and
knit 24 (30) rounds.
Shape top as first finger.
Fourth finger
RS facing, rejoin yarn A and K14 and pick up
and knit 2 sts from the base of the third finger.
Divide these 16 sts onto 3 needles and knit 20
(26) rounds.
Shape top
Round 1 *K2tog, rep from * to end.
Round 2 K to end.
Round 3 *K2tog , K1, rep from *, K2tog.

Break yarn, leaving an end to run through the sts, pull up tightly and fasten off.

Thumb

RS facing, rejoin yarn A and K18 from safety pin and pick up and knit 6 sts from base of thumb. Divide these 24 sts onto 3 needles and work 20 (24) rounds.

Shape top

Round 1 *K2tog, rep from * to end.

Round 2 K to end.

Round 3 *K2tog, rep from * to end.

Break yarn, leaving an end to run through the sts, pull up tightly and fasten off.**

LEFT GLOVE

Using 2.75mm (US 2) needles and yarn C, cast on 60 sts. Break yarn C. Join in yarn A and work cuff as for right glove. Change to st st and work 2 rounds.

Thumb gusset

Round 3 K26, inc, K2, inc, K to end.

Cont as for right glove with thumb gusset in new position.

Round 26 K25, place next 18 sts on safety pin, cast on 6 sts, K to end.

Work 20 rounds.

Divide for fingers Slip first 20 sts of round onto spare needle and rejoin yarn A with RS facing.

First finger

Work from ** to ** as on right glove.

MAKING UP

Weave in any loose ends. Press lightly using a warm iron over a damp cloth.

Rothko-style Blanket

SIZE & YARNS

Size	120 x 162cm
	47 x 64in

Rowan Handknit DK Cotton

A Green (219)	3 x 50g
B Red (215)	1 x 50g
C Pink (313)	3 x 50g
D Orange (254)	1 x 50g

NEEDLES

1 pair of 4.5mm (US 7) needles.
4mm (US G6) crochet hook.

TENSION

19 sts and 26 rows to 10cm (4in) measured
over st st using 4.5mm (US 7) needles.

BLANKET STRIP 1

Using 4.5mm (US 7) needles and yarn A, cast
on 114 sts. Break yarn A, join in yarn B and
work as folls.
Row 1 K to end.
Row 2 P to last 5 sts, K5.
These 2 rows form st st with g st edge.
Rep rows 1 and 2 until work meas 162cm
(64in), ending with row 1. Break yarn B.
Join in yarn C and purl 1 row. Cast off.

BLANKET STRIP 2

Using 4.5mm (US 7) needles and yarn A, cast
on 114 sts. Break yarn A. Join in yarn C and
work as folls.
Row 1 K to end.
Row 2 K5, P to end.
These 2 rows form st st with g st edge.
Rep rows 1 and 2 until work meas 112cm
(44in), ending with row 2. Break yarn C.
Join in yarn A and knit 2 rows. Break yarn A.
Join in yarn D and rep rows 1 and 2 until work
meas 162cm (64in), ending with row 1. Break
yarn D.
Join in yarn C and purl 1 row. Cast off.

MAKING UP

With WS together (crochet is on RS as a
contrast detail) and using 4mm (US G6)
crochet hook and yarn C, join seam with a row
of double crochet (US single crochet) to make
a decorative seam. Press lightly using a warm
iron over a damp cloth.

Rothko-style Cushion

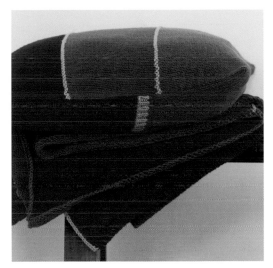

SIZE & YARNS

Size	46 x 46cm
	18 x 18in

Rowan Handknit DK Cotton

A Red (215)	3 x 50g
B Orange (254)	1 x 50g
C Pink (313)	3 x 50g
D Green (219)	1 x 50g

46 x 46cm (18 x 18in) cushion pad.

NEEDLES

1 pair each of 3.75mm (US 5) and 4mm (US 6) needles.

TENSION

20 sts and 28 rows to 10cm (4in) measured over st st using 4mm (US 6) needles.

CUSHION COVER

Using 3.75mm (US 5) needles and yarn B, cast on 91 sts. Break yarn B. Join in yarn D and work 6 rows in K1, P1 rib. Break yarn D.
Join in yarn A and change to 4mm (US 6) needles and st st. Cont until work meas 30cm (12in). Place markers at each end of last row.

Cont in st st until work meas 46cm (18in), ending with RS facing for next row.
Break yarn A.
Join in yarn D and knit 2 rows. Break yarn D.
Join in yarn B and change to st st. Cont until work meas 61cm (24in), ending with RS facing for next row. Break yarn B.
Join in yarn D and knit 2 rows. Break yarn D.
Join in yarn C and change to st st. Cont until work meas 76cm (30in). Place markers at each end of last row. Cont in st st until work meas 99cm (39in), ending with RS facing for next row. Break yarn C.
Change to 3.75mm (US 5) needles, join in yarn D and knit 1 row. Change to K1, P1 rib and work 5 rows. Break yarn D.
Join in yarn B and cast off.

MAKING UP

Place RS together, using markers as top and bottom of cushion cover, and overlap centre back of cushion cover by 10cm (4in). Stitch side seams. Turn RS out and press lightly using a warm iron over a damp cloth.
Insert cushion pad.

Beret

SIZE & YARNS

Size

To fit average head   56cm circumference.

22in circumference.

Rowan 4ply Soft

A Lavender (375)   1 x 50g

B Red (374)   Small amount for

edging.

NEEDLES

1 pair each of 2.75mm (US 2) and 3.25mm
(US 3) needles.

TENSION

28 sts and 36 rows to 10cm (4in) measured
over st st using 3.25mm (US 3) needles.

BERET

Using 2.75mm (US 2) needles and yarn B, cast
on 144 sts. Break yarn B. Join in yarn A and
work 10 rows in K1, P1 rib.
Change to 3.25mm (US 3) needles and st st.
Work as folls.
Increase row *Inc, K1, rep from * to end. 216 sts.
Work 27 rows.

Row 29 *K2tog, K4, rep from * to end. 180 sts.
Work 9 rows.
Row 39 *K2tog, K3, rep from * to end. 144 sts.
Work 7 rows.
Row 47 *K2tog, K2, rep from * to end. 108 sts.
Work 5 rows.
Row 53 *K2tog, K1, rep from * to end. 72 sts.
Work 3 rows.
Row 57 *K2tog, K4, rep from * to end. 60 sts.
Work 1 row.
Row 59 *K2tog, K3, rep from * to end. 48 sts.
Work 1 row.
Row 61 *K2tog, K2, rep from * to end. 36 sts.
Work 1 row.
Row 63 *K2tog, K1, rep from * to end. 24 sts.
Row 64 P2tog across row. 12 sts.
Break yarn, leaving thread for sewing. Thread
yarn through rem sts, pull up tightly and
secure. Weave in any loose ends.

MAKING UP

Sew seam. Press lightly using a warm iron over
a damp cloth. Place beret over a dinner plate
to dry.

Three-textured Blanket

SIZE & YARNS

Size	122 x 147cm
	48 x 58in

Rowan Cotton Glace

A Light purple (787)	10 x 50g
B Rose pink (747)	7 x 50g
C Lilac (811)	4 x 50g
D Green (814)	Small amount for edging.
E Pale lime (813)	Small amount for edging.

NEEDLES

1 pair of 3.75mm (US 5) needles.
3.75mm (US F5) crochet hook.

TENSION

23 sts and 32 rows to 10cm (4in) measured over st st using 3.75mm (US 5) needles.

BLANKET STRIP 1

Using 3.75mm (US 5) needles and yarn D, cast on 140 sts. Break yarn D, join in yarn A and knit 1 row.

Change to block patt and work as folls.

Row 1 *K5, P5, rep from * to last 10 sts, K10.
Row 2 *K5, P5, rep from * to end.
Rows 3 and 4 As rows 1 and 2.
Row 5 As row 1.
Row 6 K10,*P5, K5, rep from * to end.
Row 7 *P5, K5, rep from * to end.
Rows 8 and 9 As rows 6 and 7.
Row 10 As row 6.
Rows 1 to 10 form block patt. Cont in patt until work meas approx 147cm (58in), ending with WS facing for next row. Break yarn A.
Join in yarn E and purl 1 row.
Cast off.

BLANKET STRIP 2

Using 3.75mm (US 5) needles and yarn D, cast on 140 sts. Break yarn D. Join in yarn B and work in patt as folls.

Row 1 K to end.
Row 2 K5, P to end.
Rows 3 to 6 As rows 1 and 2, twice.
Row 7 *K3, P3, rep from * to last 8 sts, K8.
Row 8 K5, P to end.
Rows 9 to 12 As rows 7 and 8, twice.
Rows 13 to 18 As rows 1 to 6.
Row 19 *P3, K3, rep from * to last 8 sts, P3, K5.
Row 20 K5, P to end.
Rows 21 to 24 As rows 19 and 20, twice.
Rows 1 to 24 form patt rep. Cont in patt until work meas approx 101cm (40in), ending with row 4 or 16. Break yarn B.
Join in yarn E and knit 2 rows. Break yarn E.
Join in yarn C and work as folls.
Row 1 and alt rows K to end.
Row 2 K5, *K2, P4, rep from * to last 3 sts, K2, P1.
Row 4 As row 2.
Row 6 K5, P3,* K2, P4, rep from * to end.
Row 8 As row 6.
Rows 1 to 8 form patt rep. Cont in patt until work meas approx 147cm (58in), ending with row 1 or 5. Break yarn C.
Join in yarn E and purl 1 row.
Cast off.

MAKING UP

With WS together (crochet is on RS as a contrast detail) and using 3.75mm (US F5) crochet hook and yarn D, join seam with a row of double crochet (US single crochet) to make a decorative seam. Press lightly using a warm iron over a damp cloth.

CRIMSON/WINE

Rich colours and soft yarns add warmth to the cold, dark months at the end of the year, as log fires burn and as the autumn fruits gather on the trees. Deep reds and vibrant pinks blend together to create a comforting feel.

Blanket Cardigan
Wrap up for winter in this soft wool/cotton mix cardigan. Contrasting fine stripes of lime green and citrus yellow create a flash of colour. Page 48.

Following pages:
Block-striped Blanket
This blanket has an Amish patchwork feel to it, with its simple blocks of colours and stripes in Yorkshire tweed yarn. Page 52.

Tweed Slippers
Just right for toasting your feet by the fire, these Yorkshire tweed yarn slippers are knitted on two needles, and embellished with cross stitch. Page 50.

Silk Rag Rug
This very simple piece
is knitted in a tweedy
silk/cotton yarn in
garter-stitch stripes.
The soft colours give
it the feeling of a
treasured rag rug.
Page 53.

Garter-stitch Cushion
Nothing could be
simpler than this vibrant
two-tone cushion, easy
to knit on big needles in
chunky yarn. Page 54.

Block-striped Blanket
Team the cushion
opposite with the
Block-striped Blanket
(see page 36 for full
picture and page 52
for the pattern).

Child's Jacket
This soft cotton jacket is knitted with contrasting-coloured garter-stitch borders at the hem and cuffs. It can be knitted for a boy or girl, by varying the colour choice. This version is in cornflower blue with a gooseberry green trim. Page 58.

Mittens
In a raspberry-coloured wool/cotton yarn, with a citrus yellow tip to the ribs, these mittens are just right for a crisp winter's morning. Page 56.

Block-striped Scarf
Knitted in blocks of fuchsia pink and rich red, with a contrasting colour at each end, this stocking-stitch scarf is a fashionable asset to any wardrobe. Page 55.

Cable Socks
Cable-knit patterns
are great for socks
as they have extra
elasticity. Knitted in
wool/cotton yarn (the
same as the mittens),
the toes and heels
are in a rich
burgundy, while
the ribs have citrus-
yellow tips.
Page 60.

**Cable Hot-water
Bottle Cover**
This cable pattern
ensures extra
insulation and a
snug fit to the cover.
A pretty crochet picot
trim makes a nice
decorative finish,
along with the
drawstring cord in
a bright green.
Worked in cotton
yarn, it is delightfully
soft and comforting.
Page 62.

Blanket Cardigan

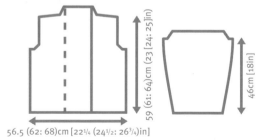

56.5 (62: 68)cm [22¼ (24½: 26¾)in]

59 (61: 64)cm [23 (24: 25)in]

46cm [18in]

SIZES & YARNS

Size	S	M	L	
To fit bust	86-96	96-107	107-117	cm
	34-38	38-42	42-46	in
Actual size	113	124	136	cm
	44½	49	53½	in
Back length	59	61	64	cm
	23	24	25	in
Sleeve Seam	46	46	46	cm
	18	18	18	in

Rowan Wool Cotton

A Burgundy (910)	17	18	19	x 50g
B Green (946)	1	1	1	x 50g
C Pale lime (901)	1	1	1	x 50g

NEEDLES

1 pair of 7.5mm (US 10½) needles.
Stitch holders.

TENSION

14 sts and 16 rows to 10cm (4in) measured over st st using 7.5mm (US 10½) needles and double (2 ends) yarn.

BACK

N.B. Use 2 ends of yarn throughout.

Using 7.5mm (US 10½) needles and yarn B, cast on 79 (87: 95) sts. Break yarn B. Join in yarn A and work 18cm (7in) in st st.

Break yarn A. Join in yarn C and work 1 row. Break yarn C. Join in yarn A and cont in st st until work meas 38 (39: 40)cm [15 (15½: 16)in], ending with RS facing for next row.

Shape armholes

Cast off 2 (3: 4) sts at beg of next 2 rows.

Row 3 K2, sl1, K1, psso, K to last 4 sts, K2tog, K2.

Row 4 P to end.

Rep rows 3 and 4 until 67 (71: 75) sts rem.

Cont without shaping until work meas 58 (60: 63)cm [23 (23½: 25)in], ending with RS facing for next row.

Shape shoulders

Cast off 9 (10: 11) sts at beg of next 4 rows.

Leave 31 sts on holder.

LEFT FRONT

Using 7.5mm (US 10½) needles and yarn B, cast on 49 (53: 57) sts. Break yarn B.

Join in yarn A and work as folls.

Row 1 K45 (49: 53), (P1, K1) twice.

Row 2 K1, P1, K1, P to end.

Rep rows 1 and 2 until work measures 18cm (7in). Break yarn A. Join in yarn C and work 1 row. Break yarn C. Join in yarn A and cont until work meas 38 (39: 40)cm [15 (15½: 16)in], ending with RS facing for next row.

Shape armhole

Row 1 Cast off 2 (3: 4) sts, patt to end.

Row 2 Patt.

Row 3 K2, sl1, K1, psso, patt to end.

Rep rows 2 and 3 until 43 (45: 47) sts rem.

Cont without shaping until work meas 58 (60: 63)cm [23 (23½: 25)in], ending with RS facing for next row.

Shape shoulder

Row 1 Cast off 9 (10: 11) sts, patt to end.

Row 2 Patt.

Rows 3 and 4 As rows 1 and 2.

Leave 25 sts on holder.

RIGHT FRONT

Work as for left front, reversing all shaping and noting **Row 1** (K1, P1) twice, K45 (49: 53).

Do NOT break yarn at end.

SLEEVES (make 2)

Using 7.5mm (US 10½) needles and yarn B, cast on 39 (41: 43) sts. Break yarn B. Join in yarn A and work in st st, inc 1 st at each end of row 11 and every foll 6th row to 59 (61: 63) sts. Cont without shaping until work meas 46cm (18In), ending with RS facing for next row.

Shape sleevehead

Rows 1 and 2 Cast off 2 (3: 4) sts, work to end.

Row 3 K2, sl1, K1, psso, K to last 4 sts, K2tog, K2.

Row 4 P to end.

Rep rows 3 and 4 until 47 sts rem.

Cast off.

COLLAR

Join shoulder seams. With RS facing and using 7.5mm (US 10½) needles and yarn A, moss st 4, K21 from right front, K31 across back, K21, then moss st 4 from left front.

Work as folls.

Row 1 Moss st 4, P to last 4 sts, moss st 4.

Row 2 Moss st 4, K17, *sl1, K1, psso, K4, K2tog,* K23, rep from * to * again, K17, moss st 4.

Row 3 As row 1.

Row 4 Moss st 4, K16, *sl1, K1, psso, K4, K2tog,* K21, rep from * to * again, K16, moss st 4.

Work decs as set on alt rows until 69 sts rem. Cont without shaping until collar measures 20cm (8in). Cast off.

MAKING UP

Join side seams. Set sleeves into armhole and stitch in place. Join underarm seams. Weave in any loose ends. Press lightly using a warm iron over a damp cloth.

Tweed Slippers

SIZES & YARNS

Size	To fit shoe size 4-5 (5-6)

Rowan Yorkshire Tweed DK

A Burgundy (342)	1 x 50g
B Rose pink (350)	2 x 50g

NEEDLES

1 pair of 3mm (US 2/3) needles.

TENSION

27 sts and 38 rows to 10cm (4in) measured over st st using 3mm (US 2/3) needles.

UPPER SIDE 1

Using 3mm (US 2/3) needles and yarn B, cast on 3 sts (toe).

Work in st st throughout.

Row 1 K to end.

Row 2 Inc 1 st at beg of row.

Row 3 Inc 1 st at each end of row.

Row 4 As row 2.

Rows 5 and 6 As rows 3 and 4.

Row 7 Inc 1 st at end of row.

Row 8 P to end.

Row 9 As row 3. 13 sts.

Shaping rows **ONLY** given from this point.

Row 13 Inc 1 st at end of row.

Row 15 Inc 1 st at beg of row.

Row 17 As row 13.

Row 21 Inc 1 st at each end of row.

Row 27 As row 15. 19 sts.

Row 31 Inc 1 st at end of row.

Row 36 Inc 1 st at beg of row.

Row 41 Inc 1 st at end of row.

Row 46 Inc 1 st at beg of row.

Row 49 Inc 1 st at end of row. 24 sts.

Cont without shaping until work meas 14.5 (15.5)cm [5½ (6)in], ending with **WS** facing for next row.

Place marker at end of last row.**

Shape opening

Row 1 P2, P2tog, P to end.

Row 2 K to last 4 sts, K2tog, K2.

Row 3 As row 1.

Row 6 As row 2.

Row 9 As row 1. 19 sts.

Cont without shaping until work meas 20 (21)cm [8 (8½)in], ending with RS facing for next row.

Next row K to last 3 sts, inc, K2.

Work 3 more rows, then rep the inc row.

Cont without shaping until work meas 24 (25)cm [9½ (10)in], ending with RS facing for next row.

Shape heel

Row 1 K to last 2 sts, yf, sl1, yb, turn.

Row 2 Sl1, P to last 2 sts, P2tog.

Row 3 K to last 4 sts, yf, sl1, yb, turn.

Row 4 Sl1, P to last 2 sts, P2tog.

Cast off.

UPPER SIDE 2

Work as for side 1 to **, but reversing shaping, i.e. row 2 reads inc 1 st at END of row and row 7 reads inc 1 st at BEG of row.

Shape opening

Row 1 P to last 4 sts, P2tog tbl, P2.

Row 2 K2, sl1, K1, psso, K to end.

Row 3 As row 1.

Row 6 As row 2.

Row 9 As row 1. 19 sts.

Cont without shaping until work meas 20 (21)cm [8 (8½)in], ending with RS facing for next row.

Next row K1, inc, K to end.

Work 3 more rows, then rep the inc row.

Cont without shaping until work meas 24

(25)cm [9½ (10)in], ending with RS facing for next row.

Shape heel

Row 1 K to end

Row 2 P2tog, P to last 2 sts, yb, sl1, yf, turn.

Row 3 Sl1, K to end.

Row 4 P2tog, P to last 4 sts, yb, sl1, yf, turn.

Row 5 Sl1, K to end.

Cast off purlwise.

SOLE

Using 3mm (US 2/3) needles and yarn A, cast on 7 sts (heel).

Work in st st throughout.

Row 1 K to end.

Rows 2 and 3 Cast on 2 sts at beg of row.

Row 4 Inc 1 st at each end of row.

Shaping rows **ONLY** given from this point.

Rows 7, 10 and 13 Inc 1 st at each end or row. 19 sts.

Cont without shaping until work meas 7cm (3in).

Dec 1 st at each end of next and foll 4th row.

Cont without shaping until work meas 13cm (5in), ending with RS facing for next row.

Row 1 Inc 1 st at each end of row.

Rows 7, 13, 17 and 21 As row 1. 25 sts.

Cont without shaping until work meas 20 (21)cm [8 (8½)in].

Shape toe

Row 1 Dec 1 st at at each end of row.

Rows 4, 7, 10, 13, 15 and 16 As row 1. 11 sts.

Rows 17 and 18 Cast off 2 sts at beg of row, work to end.

Cast off rem 7 sts.

MAKING UP

Place WS of uppers together and, using yarn B and starting at marker, join seam to toe with a running stitch 5mm (¼in) from edge, then return to marker using the same holes and forming a decorative seam. Using yarn A, work cross stitch over the seam (see photograph).

Join heel seam 5mm (¼in) from edge as before, omitting cross stitch.

Carefully pin upper to sole, WS facing, easing around heel and toe. Stitch as before.

Make second slipper to match.

Block-striped Blanket

SIZE & YARNS

Size	120 x 165cm
	47 x 65in

Rowan Yorkshire Tweed DK

A Rose pink (350)	6 x 50g
B Pale lime (348)	3 x 50g
C Burgundy (342)	3 x 50g
D Green (349)	3 x 50g
E Red (344)	10 x 50g

NEEDLES

1 pair of 4mm (US 6) needles.
4mm (US G6) crochet hook.

TENSION

20 sts and 28 rows to 10cm (4in) measured
over st st using 4mm (US 6) needles.

BLANKET STRIP 1

Using 4mm (US 6) needles and yarn D, cast on
132 sts. Break yarn D. Join in yarn E and work
as folls.
Row 1 K to end.
Row 2 K5, P to end.
These 2 rows form st st with g st edge.

Rep rows 1 and 2 until work meas 117cm
(46in).
Break yarn E. Join in yarn D and work 1 row.
Break yarn D. Join in yarn A and cont in patt
until work meas 165cm (65in), ending with WS
facing for next row.
Break yarn A. Join in yarn B and work 1 row.
Cast off.

BLANKET STRIP 2

Using 4mm (US 6) needles and yarn D, cast on
132 sts. Break yarn D. Join in yarn A and work
as folls.
Row 1 K to end.
Row 2 P to last 5 sts, K5.
These 2 rows form st st with g st edge.
Rep rows 1 and 2, working in 13cm (5in)
stripes of yarns A, B, C, D and E until work
meas 165cm (65in), ending with WS facing for
next row.
Break yarn. Join in yarn B and work 1 row.
Cast off.

MAKING UP

With WS together (crochet is on RS as a
contrast detail) and using 4mm (US G6)
crochet hook and yarn E, join seam with a row
of double crochet (US single crochet) to make
decorative seam. Press lightly using a warm
iron over a damp cloth.

Silk Rag Rug

SIZE & YARNS

Size	55cm wide x 97cm long
	21½in wide x 38in long

Rowan Summer Tweed

A Pale grey (506)	3 x 50g
B Light blue (500)	3 x 50g
C Lime green (527)	3 x 50g
D Light purple (525)	3 x 50g
E Fuchsia (528)	3 x 50g

NEEDLES

1 pair of 5mm (US 8) needles.
Medium size crochet hook.

TENSION

16 sts and 32 rows to 10cm (4in) measured
over garter stitch using 5mm (US 8) needles.

SPECIAL NOTES

1. Rug is worked in garter stitch throughout.
2. When changing colours, knit in the ends.
3. Vary the number of stitches for change
position.

RUG

Using 5mm (US 8) needles and yarn A, cast on
88 sts and work in g st in colour and row
sequence as folls.

Row rep is *2 rows plus a few stitches of first
colour, 4 rows plus a few stitches of second
colour, then 6 rows plus a few stitches of third
colour. Rep from *.

Colour rep is *yarn A, yarn B, yarn C, yarn D,
then yarn E. Rep from *.

Cont until work meas 97cm (38in). Cast off.

MAKING UP

Press using a warm iron over a damp cloth.

Make fringe

Cut 3 lengths of yarn 25cm (10in) long, fold in
half and use a crochet hook to pull the loop
through the end of the rug. Tuck the ends of
the tassel through the loop and pull tight.
Make 6 tassels in each colour and place them
in A to E sequence in every 3rd stitch. Repeat
for other end of rug.

Garter-stitch Cushion

SIZE & YARNS

Size	46 x 46cm
	18 x 18in

Rowan Polar

A Red (641)	2 x 100g
B Fuchsia (651)	2 x 100g

46 x 46cm (18 x 18in) cushion pad.

NEEDLES

1 pair of 8mm (US 11) needles.

TENSION

12 sts and 16 rows to 10cm (4in) measured over st st using 8mm (US 11) needles.

CUSHION COVER

Using 8mm (US 11) needles and yarn A, cast on 56 sts. Join in yarn B and work 3 rows in K1, P1 rib. Break yarn B.

Using yarn A, change to st st. Cont in st st until work meas 25cm (10in). Place markers at each end of last row. Cont in st st until work measures 48cm (19in), ending with RS facing for next row. Break yarn A. Join in yarn B and change to g st.

Cont in g st until work meas 71cm (28in). Place markers at each end of row. Cont in g st until work meas 99cm (39in), ending with WS facing for next row.

Join in yarn A and purl 1 row. Change to K1, P1 rib and work 2 rows. Break yarn A.

Using yarn B, cast off in rib.

MAKING UP

Place RS together, using markers as top and bottom of cushion cover, and overlap centre back of cushion cover by 10cm (4in). Stitch side seams. Turn RS out and press lightly using a warm iron over a damp cloth. Insert cushion pad.

Block-striped Scarf

SIZE & YARNS

Size	Length	Width	
	137	30	cm
	54	12	in

Rowan 4ply Soft

A Red (374)	3 x 50g	
B Pink (377)	1 x 50g	
C Light green (379)	Small amount for edging detail.	
D Lavender (375)	Small amount for edging detail.	

NEEDLES

1 pair of 3.25mm (US 3) needles

TENSION

28 sts and 36 rows to 10cm (4in) measured over st st using 3.25mm (US 3) needles.

SCARF

Using 3.25mm (US 3) needles and yarn C, cast on 84 sts. Break yarn C. Join in yarn A and work as folls.

Row 1 K to end.

Row 2 K6, P to last 6 sts, K6.

Rep rows 1 and 2 until work meas 101cm (40in), ending with row 2. Break yarn A.

Next row Join in yarn C and work as row 1. Break yarn C.

Next row Join in yarn B and work as row 2. Cont with yarn B until work meas 137cm (54in), ending with row 2. Break yarn B. Join in yarn D and cast off.

MAKING UP

Weave in any loose ends. Press lightly using a warm iron over a damp cloth.

Mittens

SIZES & YARNS

Size	S-M	M-L	

Rowan Wool Cotton

A Rose pink (943)	2	2	x 50g
B Pale lime (901)	Small amount for edging.		

NEEDLES

1 pair of 3.25mm (US 3) needles.
Cable needle.

TENSION

24 sts and 32 rows to 10cm (4in) measured
over st st using 3.25mm (US 3) needles.

RIGHT MITTEN

Cuff

Using 3.25mm (US 3) needles and yarn B, cast
on 52 sts. Break yarn B. Join in yarn A and
work twisted rib as folls.

Row 1 *P1 K2tog, do NOT slip stitch off needle
but knit into first stitch again, then slip both
stitches off needle, P1, rep from * to end.

Row 2 *K1, P2, K1, rep from * to end.

Rows 3 to 14 As rows 1 and 2, six times.

Row 15 As row 1.

Row 16 (*K1, P2, K1, rep from * once, K1, P2tog
K1), 4 times, K1, P2, K1. 48 sts.
Change to st st and work 4 rows.**

Shape gusset for thumb

Row 1 K25, pick up loop of row below and knit
into the back of it (called **mk**), K2, mk, K21.
Work 2 rows.

Row 4 P21, pick up loop of row below and purl
into the back of it (called **mp**), P4, mp, P25.
Work 2 rows.

Cont inc 2 sts on every 3rd row, working 2
extra sts between inc to row 19, (K25, mk, K14,
mk, K21). 62 sts.
Work 3 rows.

Shape thumb

Row 1 K41, turn.

Row 2 Cast on 1 st , P17, turn.

Row 3 Cast on 1 st , K18, turn.

Cont on these 18 sts until thumb meas 5cm
(2in), ending with RS facing for next row.

Next row *K1, K2tog, rep from* to end.

Next row P to end.

Next row K2tog across row.

Break yarn and thread through rem sts. Pull up
tightly and secure. Sew thumb seam.
With RS facing, rejoin yarn to base of thumb.

Pick up and knit 2 sts from cast-on sts at base
of thumb, knit across rem 21 sts. 48 sts.
***Cont in st st until work meas 13 (15)cm [5
(6)in] from top of cable rib, ending with RS
facing for next row.

Shape top

Row 1 *Sl1, K1, psso, K20, K2tog, rep from *.

Row 2 P to end.

Row 3 *Sl1, K1, psso, K18, K2tog, rep from *.

Row 4 P to end.

Cont dec as set on alt rows until 24 sts rem.
Work 1 row. Cast off.
Sew top and side seam.***

LEFT MITTEN

Cast on and work to ** as for right mitten.

Shape gusset for thumb

Row 1 K21, mk, K2, mk, K25.
Work 2 rows.

Row 4 P25, mp, P4, mp, P21.
Work 2 rows.

Cont inc as set to row 19 (K21, mk, K14, mk,
K25). 62 sts.
Work 3 rows.

Shape thumb

Row 1 K37, turn.

Row 2 Cast on 1 st, P17, turn.

Row 3 Cast on 1 st, K18, turn.

Complete thumb as for right mitten.

With RS facing, rejoin yarn to base of thumb.

Pick up and knit 2 sts from cast on sts at base

of thumb, knit across rem 25 sts. 48 sts.

Work from *** to *** as on right mitten.

MAKING UP

Press lightly using a warm iron over a

damp cloth.

Child's Jacket

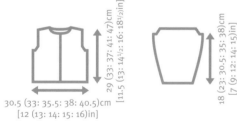

30.5 (33: 35.5: 38: 40.5)cm
[12 (13: 14: 15: 16)in]

29 (33: 37: 41: 47)cm
[11.5 (13: 14½: 16: 18½)in]

18 (23: 30.5: 35: 38)cm
[7 (9: 12: 14: 15)in]

SIZES & YARNS

	1-2	3-4	5-6	7-8	9-10	years
To fit						
chest	56	61	66	71	76	cm
	22	24	26	28	30	in
Actual						
size	61	66	71	76	81	cm
	24	26	28	30	32	in
Back						
length	29	33	37	41	47	cm
	11½	13	14½	16	18½	in
Sleeve						
seam	18	23	30.5	35	38	cm
	7	9	12	14	15	in

Rowan Handknit DK Cotton

A Blue (287)

	4	5	5	6	7	x 50g

B Green (219)

	1	1	1	1	1	x 50g

Buttons	5	5	5	7	7

NEEDLES

1 pair each of 3.25mm (US 3) and 4mm (US 6) needles.

2 safety pins.

TENSION

20 sts and 28 rows to 10cm (4in) measured over st st using 4mm (US 6) needles.

BACK

Using 3.25mm (US 3) needles and yarn B, cast on 60 (65: 70: 75: 80) sts.

Knit 5 (5: 7: 7: 7) rows.

Break yarn B. Join in yarn A and change to 4mm (US 6) needles and st st.

Cont until work meas 17 (19: 21: 23: 25)cm [6½ (7½: 8½: 9: 10)in], ending with RS facing for next row.

Shape armholes

Cast off 2 (2: 3: 3: 4) sts at beg of next 2 rows.

Dec 1 st at each end of next and foll alt rows until 52 (55: 58: 61: 64) sts rem. Cont without shaping until work meas 28 (32: 36: 40: 46)cm [11 (12½: 14: 15½: 18)in], ending with RS facing for next row.

Shape shoulders

Sizes 1 and 2

Cast off 16 (17) sts at beg of next 2 rows.

Cast off.

Sizes 3, 4 and 5

Cast off 6 (6: 7) sts at beg of next 4 rows.

Cast off 6 (7: 6) sts at beg of next 2 rows.

Cast off.

LEFT FRONT

Using 3.25mm (US 3) needles and yarn B, cast on 34 (36: 38: 41: 43) sts.

Knit 5 (5: 7: 7: 7) rows.

Break yarn B. Join in yarn A and change to 4mm (US 6) needles and st st.

Row 1 K30 (32: 34: 37: 39), leave last 4 sts on safety pin.

Cont in st st until work measures 17 (19: 21: 23: 25)cm [6½ (7½: 8½: 9: 10)in], ending with RS facing for next row.

Shape armhole

Cast off 2 (2: 3: 3: 4) sts, K to end.

Purl 1 row.

Dec 1 st at beg of next and foll alt rows until 26 (27: 28: 30: 31) sts rem.

Cont without shaping until work is 11 (11: 7: 7: 9) rows LESS than back at shoulder, ending with **WS** facing for next row.

Shape neck

Sizes 1 and 2

Row 1 (WS) Cast off 5 sts, work to end.

Rows 2 to 5 Dec 1 st at neck edge.

Row 6 K to end.

Row 7 Dec 1 st at neck edge.

Rows 8 to 11 St st.

Cast off.

Sizes 3, 4 and 5

Row 1 Cast off 5 (6: 6) sts, work to end.

Rows 2 to 5 Dec 1 st at neck edge.

Row 6 K to end.

Row 7 Dec 1 st at neck edge.

Size 5 ONLY work 2 rows in st st.

Shape shoulder

Cast off 6 (6: 7) sts at beg of next and foll alt row.

Work 1 row. Cast off rem 6 (7: 6) sts.

RIGHT FRONT

Work as for left front, reversing all shaping and starting neck 10 (10: 6: 6: 8) rows LESS than back at shoulder.

SLEEVES (make 2)

Using 3.25mm (US 3) needles and yarn B, cast on 33 (35: 37: 40: 42) sts and knit 5 (5: 7: 7: 7) rows. Break yarn B. Join in yarn A and change to 4mm (US 6) needles and st st.

Inc 1 st at each end of 5th and every foll 4th (4th: 5th: 6th 6th) row to 53 (55: 59: 60: 64) sts.

Cont without shaping until work meas 18 (23: 30.5: 35: 38)cm [7 (9: 12: 14: 15)in], ending with RS facing for next row.

Shape sleevehead

Cast off 2 (2: 3: 3: 4) sts at beg of next 2 rows. Dec 1 st at each end of next and foll alt rows until 45 (45: 47: 46: 48) sts rem. Cast off loosely.

BUTTON BAND

Using 3.25mm (US 3) needles and yarn A and with RS of left front facing, pick up loop before 4 sts on safety pin and K into back of it, K across 4 sts on safety pin. Work in K1, P1 rib until band, when slightly stretched, fits to neck of left front. Cast off. Sew band to left front. Mark positions for buttons, the first 1cm (½in) from neck, the remainder at regular intervals, ending before the garter-stitch hem.

BUTTONHOLE BAND

Work as for button band, rejoining yarn with WS facing and purling across row. Make buttonholes by rib 1, K2tog, yon, rib 2, to

correspond with marked button positions. Sew band to right front.

COLLAR

Using 3.25mm (US 3) needles and yarn A, cast on 55 (57: 61: 65: 71) sts and work in g st for 5.5 (5.5: 6: 6.5: 7)cm [2 (2: 2½: 2½: 2¾)in]. Cast off.

MAKING UP

Join shoulder and side seams. Join sleeve seams. Starting and finishing halfway across front bands, pin cast-off edge of collar around neck, RS of collar to WS of garment. Sew into place. Weave in any loose ends. Pin sleeves to body, centre of sleeve top to shoulder seam, and stitch into place. Sew on buttons. Press lightly using a warm iron over a damp cloth.

Cable Socks

SIZES & YARNS

To fit	S - M	M - L	
Foot length	24	26	cm
	9½	10¼	in

Rowan Wool Cotton

A Dusty pink (959)	4	4	x 50g
B Burgundy (910)	1	1	x 50g
C Pale lime (901)	Small amount for		
	edging.		

NEEDLES

4 x 4mm (US 6) double-ended needles.
Spare needle. Cable needle.

TENSION

22 sts and 30 rows to 10cm (4in) measured
over st st using 4mm (US 6) needles.

SPECIAL ABBREVIATIONS

c4b = place next 2 sts on cable needle, leave
at back of work, K2, K2 from cable needle.

SOCKS

Using 4mm (US 6) needles and yarn C, cast on
60 sts (20 sts on each of 3 needles). Break
yarn C. Join in yarn B and work 6 rounds in K1,
P1 rib. Break yarn B.

Join in yarn A and work as folls.

Rounds 1 to 4 *P2, K4, P2, K2, rep from * to end.

Round 5 *P2, c4b, P2 K2, rep from * to end.

Round 6 As round 1.

Rep rounds 1 to 6 until work meas approx
33cm (13in), ending with round 6.

Next round P2, K1, K2tog, K1, P2, K2, *P2, K4,
P2, K2, rep from * twice more, *P2, K1, K2tog,
K1, P2, K2, rep from *. 57 sts.

Start heel

P2, K3, P2, K2. Break yarn A. Turn. Using
spare needle and joining in yarn B (WS facing),
P29, turn.

On these 29 sts, work 6cm (2½in) in st st,
ending with RS facing for next row.

Shape heel

Row 1 K16, K2tog tbl, K1, turn.

Row 2 Sl1, P5, P2tog, P1, turn.

Row 3 Sl1, K6, K2tog tbl, K1, turn.

Row 4 Sl1, P7, P2tog, P1, turn.

Cont as set until all sts are on 1 needle. Break
yarn B.

Next row With RS facing, using needle 1 and
joining in yarn A, pick up 10 sts from side of
heel, K8 from spare needle, with needle 2, K9
from spare needle, pick up 10 sts from side
of heel, with needle 3, patt 28 sts from
instep. 65 sts.

Work in rounds as folls.

Round 1 K2, sl1, K1, psso, K to last 4 sts of
needle 2, K2tog, K2, patt across needle 3.

Round 2 Work across sts.

Rep rounds 1 and 2 until 53 sts rem.

Cont without shaping until foot meas 19
(21)cm [7½ (8¼)in]. Break yarn A.

Shape toe

Join in yarn B.

Round 1 K28, *K2tog, K8, rep from *, K2tog,
K3. 50 sts.

Round 2 *K2, sl1, K1, psso, K17, K2tog, K2, rep
from *.

Rounds 3 and 4 Work across all sts.

Round 5 *K2, sl1, K1, psso, K15, K2tog, K2, rep
from *.

Rounds 6 and 7 Work across all sts.

Round 8 *K2, sl1, K1, psso, K13, K2tog, K2, rep
from *.

Rounds 9 and 10 Work across all sts.

Round 11 *K2, sl1, K1, psso, K11, K2tog, K2, rep
from *.

Round 12 Work across all sts.

Round 13 *K2, sl1, K1, psso, K9, K2tog, K2, rep from *.

Round 14 Work across all sts.

Round 15 *K2, sl1, K1, psso, K7, K2tog, K2, rep from *.

Round 16 Work across all sts.

Cast off.

Make second sock to match.

MAKING UP

Oversew cast-off edge to make a flat seam.
Weave in any loose ends. Press lightly using a
warm iron over a damp cloth.

Hot-water Bottle Cover

SIZE & YARNS

Size	To fit average size hot-water bottle.

Rowan Handknit DK Cotton

A Lilac (305)	4 x 50g
B Green (219)	1 x 50g

NEEDLES

1 pair of 4mm (US 6) needles.

TENSION

20 sts and 28 rows to 10cm (4in) measured over st st using 4mm (US 6) needles.

SPECIAL ABBREVIATIONS

c6b = place next 3 sts on cable needle, leave at back of work, K3, K3 from cable needle.

COVER PART 1

Using 4mm (US 6) needles and yarn B, cast on 49 sts. Break yarn B. Join in yarn A and work 4 rows in K1, P1 rib.

Next row (RS) P2, *P3, inc, K1, inc, K1, rep from * to last 5 sts, P5. 61 sts.

Change to patt as folls.

Row 1 and alt rows K2, *K3, P6, rep from * to last 5 sts, K5.

Row 2 P2, *P3, K6, rep from * to last 5 sts, P5.

Row 4 P2, *P3, c6b, rep from *to last 5 sts, P5.

Row 6 As row 2.

Rows 1 to 6 form patt rep. Cont in patt until work meas 39cm (15½in), ending with RS facing for next row.

Shape shoulders

Row 1 K2, sl1, K1, psso, patt to last 4 sts, K2tog, K2.

Row 2 P2, P2tog, patt to last 4 sts, P2tog tbl, P2.

Row 3 K2, sl1, K1, psso, K1, K2tog, patt to last 7 sts, sl1, K1, psso, K1, K2tog, K2.

Row 4 As row 2.

Row 5 K2, sl1, K1, psso, K2tog, patt to last 6 sts, sl1, K1, psso, K2tog, K2.

Row 6 As row 2.

Row 7 K2, sl1, K1, psso, patt to last 4 sts, K2tog, K2.

Row 8 As row 2.

Row 9 As row 7.

Row 10 As row 2.

Row 11 K2, sl1, K1, psso, K1, K2tog, patt to last 7 sts, sl1, K1, psso, K1, K2tog, K2.

Row 12 P2, P2tog, P2tog tbl, patt to last 6 sts, P2tog, P2tog tbl, P2.

Row 13 As row 7.

Row 14 P2, P2tog, P3, P2tog, P1, P2tog, P4, P2tog, P1, P2tog, P2, P2tog tbl, P2. 21 sts.

Row 15 K to end.

Row 16 (make eyelet holes) P1, *P2tog, yon, P2, rep from * to end.

Work 16 rows in st st. Cast off.

COVER PART 2

Work as for cover part 1 until knitting meas 19cm (7½in), ending with same patt row as on part 1 and with RS facing for next row.

Shape shoulders as on part 1.

MAKING UP

Place RS together, matching shoulders and top. Fold extension of part 1 up to part 2 and overlap part 2 by 6cm (2½in). Sew side seams. Turn RS out and press using a warm iron over a damp cloth.

Make picot edging around top as folls.

Using yarn B, work a round of double crochet (US single crochet) around top.

Next round *1dc in each of next 3dc, then work

3ch and join with a slip st to last dc to make
picot, rep from * to end.
Make drawstring by cutting 6 lengths of yarn
B, 130cm (51in) long. Tie lengths together with
a knot 7cm (3in) from one end. Make a plait,
using 2 ends for each strand. Tie knot at
finishing end, leaving 7cm (3in) free. Thread
through eyelets of cover.

CHARCOAL/SLATE

This largely monochrome colour palette reflects the clear silhouettes of the winter landscape. The minimalist look is softened by the use of luxury yarns with interesting textures. Protect against the weather with warm sweaters, soft blankets and cosy cushions.

Tweed sweater (opposite)

This comfortable polo-neck sweater with cable ribs is great for everyone, of any age, male or female.
Page 76.

Left: The Wrap Cardigan (also shown on page 71) and the Half-and-half and Folding Cushions (shown on pages 72 and 73) are great for winter picnics on the beach.

Half-and-half and Tweed Blankets
Two versatile blankets to knit: use them as throws, covers or winter wraps. The Half-and-half Blanket (far left and opposite) is knitted in two pieces and grafted together using a simple crochet stitch. The Tweed Blanket (left) is knitted in two shades of knobbly grey Yorkshire tweed yarn, trimmed in black.

Wrap cardigan (page 71)
This is a versatile garment; dress it up with a white lacy antique blouse, or wrap it around you for a walk on the beach. Page 80.

Half-and-half Cushion

A simple but very graphic cushion design, knitted in two colours of a wool/cotton yarn, with a rib closure providing a feature on the reverse side. Page 84.

Folding Cushion

One of the easiest designs to knit, this soft, fluffy mohair cushion goes well with the Half-and-half Cushion. Page 83.

Tweed Cushion
A single row of contrasting colour sets off the monochrome blocks of colour on this warm wool cushion. Page 82.

Half-and-half and Tweed Blankets
Seeing them close up, you can appreciate the textural qualities of these wonderfully graphic blankets. See also pages 68 and 69, and patterns on pages 78 and 79.

Tweed Sweater

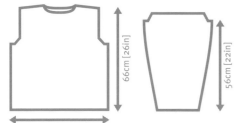

56 (61: 66)cm [22 (24: 26)in]

66cm [26in]

56cm [22in]

SIZES & YARNS

Size	S	M	L	
To fit chest	102	112	122	cm
	40	44	48	in
Actual size	112	122	132	cm
	44	48	52	in
Back length	66	66	66	cm
	26	26	26	in
Sleeve seam	56	56	56	cm
	22	22	22	in

Rowan Yorkshire Tweed 4ply

A Mid grey (270)	26	28	30	x 25g
B Charcoal grey (277)	1	1	1	x 25g

NEEDLES

1 pair each of 4.5mm (US 7) and 5mm (US 8) needles.
Cable needle.

TENSION

19 sts and 26 rows to 10cm (4in) measured over st st using 5mm (US 8) needles and double (2 ends) yarn.

SPECIAL ABBREVIATIONS

c4b = place next 2 sts on cable needle, leave at back of work, K2, K2 from cable needle.

BACK

N.B. Use 2 ends of yarn throughout.

Using 4.5mm (US 7) needles and yarn B, cast on 106 (116: 126) sts. Break yarn B and join in yarn A.

Work in cable rib as folls.

Row 1 P1 (0: K2),*P2, K4, rep from * to last 3 (2: 4) sts, P2, P1 (0: K2).

Row 2 K1 (0: P2), *K2, P4, rep from * to last 3 (2: 4) sts, K2, K1 (0: P2).

Rows 3 and 4 As rows 1 and 2.

Row 5 P1 (0: K2), *P2, c4b, rep from * to last 3 (2: 4) sts, P2, P1 (0: K2).

Row 6 As row 2.

Rows 1 to 6 form cable rib patt.

Rows 7 to 18 As rows 1 to 6, twice.

Change to 5mm (US 8) needles and st st. Cont until work measures 41cm (16in).

Shape armholes

Rows 1 and 2 Cast off 3 (3: 4) sts, work to end.

Row 3 K2, sl1, K1, psso, K to last 4 sts, K2tog, K2.

Row 4 P to end.

Rep rows 3 and 4 until 94 (102: 108) sts rem.

Cont without shaping until work meas 64cm (25in).

Shape shoulders and neck

Rows 1 and 2 Cast off 8 (8: 9) sts, K to end.

Row 3 Cast off 8 (8: 9) sts, K19 (23: 24), turn.

Row 4 Cast off 4 sts, P to end.

Row 5 Cast off 8 (9: 9) sts, K to end.

Row 6 Cast off 0 (1: 2) sts, P to end.

Cast off.

Place centre 24 sts on stitch holder. RS facing, rejoin yarn to rem sts at neck edge and work to match, reversing shaping.

FRONT

Work as for back until front meas 61.5cm (24in).

Shape neck

Row 1 K38 (41: 43), turn.

Rows 2 to 5 Dec 1 st at neck edge.

Row 6 P to end.

Row 7 Cast off 8 (8: 9) sts, K to last 2 sts, K2tog.

Row 8 P to end.

Rows 9 and 10 As rows 7 and 8.

Row 11 Cast off 8 (9: 9) sts, work to last 2 sts, K2tog.

Row 12 P to end.

Cast off.

Place centre 18 (20: 22) sts on stitch holder. RS facing, rejoin yarn to rem sts and work to match first side of neck, reversing shaping.

SLEEVES (make 2)

Using yarn B and 4.5mm (US 7) needles, cast on 50 (50: 56) sts. Break yarn B and join in yarn A. Work 18 rows in cable rib as for 2nd (medium) size back.

Change to 5mm (US 8) needles and st st. Inc 1 st at each end of every foll 6th row to 86 (86: 88) sts. Cont without shaping until work meas 56cm (22in).

Shape sleevehead

Cast off 3 (3: 4) sts at beg of next 2 rows.

Row 3 K2, sl1, K1, psso, K to last 4 sts, K2tog, K2.

Row 4 P to end.

Rep rows 3 and 4 until 64 sts rem. Cast off.

POLO-NECK COLLAR

Join right shoulder seam. With RS facing and using 4.5mm (US 7) needles and yarn A, pick up and K15 sts down left front neck, knit across

18 (20: 22) sts on holder, pick up and K15 sts up right front neck, K6 (7: 8) sts from right back neck, knit across 24 sts on holder, pick up and K6 (7: 8) sts from left back neck. 84 (88: 92) sts.

Work 18cm (7in) in K2, P2 rib. Cast off loosely in rib.

MAKING UP

Join left shoulder and collar seam (remember that it folds over). Join side and sleeve seams. Ease sleevehead into armhole and stitch into place.

Half-and-half Blanket

SIZE & YARNS

Size	120 x 162cm
	47 x 64in

Rowan Wool Cotton

A Grey (903)	10 x 50g
B Black (908)	10 x 50g

NEEDLES

1 pair of 4mm (US 6) needles.

4mm (US G6) crochet hook.

TENSION

22 sts and 30 rows to 10cm (4in) measured over st st using 4mm (US 6) needles.

BLANKET STRIP 1

Using 4mm (US 6) needles and yarn A, cast on 132 sts. Break yarn A. Join in yarn B and work as folls.

Row 1 (K1, P1) twice, K to end.

Row 2 P to last 5 sts, (K1, P1) twice, K1.

These 2 rows form st st with moss st edge.

Rep rows 1 and 2 until work meas 162cm (64in), ending with row 2 and RS facing for next row. Cast off.

BLANKET STRIP 2

Using 4mm (US 6) needles and yarn A, cast on 132 sts.

Row 1 K to last 5 sts, (P1, K1) twice, P1.

Row 2 (P1, K1) twice, P to end.

These 2 rows form st st with moss st edge.

Rep rows 1 and 2 until work is 1 row less than strip 1 at cast-off edge, ending with WS facing for next row. Break yarn A.

Join in yarn B and work row 2. Cast off.

MAKING UP

With WS together (crochet is on RS as a contrast detail) and using 4mm (US G6) crochet hook and yarn A, join seam with a row of double crochet (US single crochet) to make decorative seam. Press lightly using a warm iron over a damp cloth.

Tweed Blanket

SIZE & YARNS

Size	131 x 172cm
	51 x 68in

Rowan Yorkshire Tweed 4ply

A Charcoal grey (277)	34 x 25g
B Mid grey (270)	16 x 25g
C Black (283)	1 x 25g

NEEDLES

1 pair of 5mm (US 8) needles.
4mm (US G6) crochet hook.

TENSION

19 sts and 26 rows to 10cm (4in) measured
over st st using 5mm (US 8) needles and
double (2 ends) yarn.

BLANKET STRIP 1

N.B. Use 2 ends of yarn throughout.
Using 5mm (US 8) needles and yarn B, cast on
124 sts. Break yarn B. Join in yarn A and work
as folls.
Row 1 K to end.
Row 2 P to last 5 sts, K5.
These 2 rows form st st with g st edge.

Cont as set until work meas 122cm (48in),
ending with row 1. Break yarn A.
Join in yarn C and work row 2. Break yarn C.
Join in yarn B and rep rows 1 and 2 until work
meas 172cm (68in), ending with row 1. Break
yarn B.
Join in yarn C and purl 1 row.
Cast off.

BLANKET STRIP 2

Using 5mm (US 8) needles and yarn B, cast on
124 sts. Break yarn B, join in yarn A and work
colours as for strip 1 but note:
Row 1 K to end.
Row 2 K5, P to end.
Work as strip 1.

MAKING UP

With WS together (crochet is on RS as a
contrast detail) and using 2 ends of yarn A and
4mm (US G6) crochet hook, join seam with a
row of double crochet (US single crochet) to
make decorative seam. Press lightly using a
warm iron over a damp cloth.

Wrap Cardigan

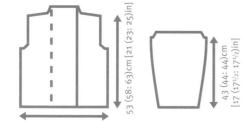

50.5 (56: 60.5)cm [20 (19³/₄: 23³/₄)in]

53 (58: 63)cm [21 (23: 25)in]

43 (44: 44)cm [17 (17¹/₂: 17¹/₂)in]

SIZES & YARNS

Size	S	M	L	
To fit bust	86-91	91-96	102-112	cm
	34-36	36-38	40-44	in
Actual size	101	112	121	cm
	39¹/₂	44	47¹/₂	in
Back length	53	58	63	cm
	21	23	25	in
Sleeve Seam	43	44	44	cm
	17	17¹/₂	17¹/₂	in

Rowan Wool Cotton

A Black (908)	10	11	12	x 50g
B Grey (903)	1	1	1	x 50g

NEEDLES

1 pair of 4mm (US 6) needles.
Stitch holder.

TENSION

22 sts and 30 rows to 10cm (4in) measured over st st using 4mm (US 6) needles.

BACK

Using 4mm (US 6) needles and yarn B, cast on 111 (123: 133) sts.

Break yarn B and join in yarn A.
Work 45 rows in st st.
Break yarn A. Join in yarn B and purl 1 row.
Break yarn B. Join in yarn A and cont in st st until work meas 32 (36: 40)cm [12¹/₂ (14: 15¹/₂)in].

Shape armholes

Cast off 3 (4: 5) sts at beg of next 2 rows.
Row 3 K2, sl1, K1, psso, K to last 4 sts, K2tog, K2.
Row 4 P to end.
Rep rows 3 and 4 until 95 (103: 109) sts rem.
Cont without shaping until work meas 52 (57: 62)cm [20¹/₂ (22¹/₂: 24¹/₂)in], ending with RS facing for next row.

Shape shoulders

Rows 1 to 4 Cast off 8 (9: 10) sts, work to end.
Rows 5 and 6 Cast off 7 (8: 9) sts, work to end.
Leave rem 49 (51: 51) sts on holder.

LEFT FRONT

Using 4mm (US 6) needles and yarn B, cast on 73 (78: 83) sts.
Break yarn B.
Join in yarn A and work as folls.
Row 1 K68 (73: 78), (P1, K1) twice, P1.

Row 2 (P1, K1) twice, P to end.
Rows 1 and 2 form st st with moss st border.
Rows 3 to 44 As rows 1 and 2.
Row 45 As row 1.
Break yarn A.
Row 46 Join in yarn B, as row 2.
Break yarn B.
Join in yarn A and cont in st st with moss st edging until work measures 32 (36: 40)cm [12¹/₂ (14: 15¹/₂)in], ending with RS facing for next row.

Shape armhole

Row 1 Cast off 3 (4: 5) sts, patt to end.
Row 2 Patt to end.
Row 3 K2, sl1, K1, psso, patt to end.
Rep rows 2 and 3 until 65 (68: 71) sts rem.
Cont without shaping until work meas 52 (57: 62)cm [20¹/₂ (22¹/₂: 24¹/₂)in], ending with RS facing for next row.

Shape shoulder

Row 1 Cast off 8 (9: 10) sts, patt to end.
Rows 2 Patt to end.
Rows 3 and 4 As rows 1 and 2.
Row 5 Cast off 7 (8: 9) sts, patt to end.
Row 6 Patt to end.
Leave rem 42 sts on holder.

RIGHT FRONT

Work as for left front, reversing all shaping and OMITTING the row in yarn B. Do NOT break yarn at end.

SLEEVES (make 2)

Using 4mm (US 6) needles and yarn B, cast on 51 (55: 61) sts. Break yarn B. Join in yarn A. Change to st st and inc 1 st at each end of row 7 and every foll 8th row to 79 (83: 87) sts. Cont until work measures 43 (44: 44)cm [17 (17½: 17½)in], ending with RS facing for next row.

Shape sleevehead

Rows 1 and 2 Cast off 3 (4: 5) sts, work to end.
Work decs as on back until 63 (69: 71) sts rem.
Work 1 row.
Cast off.

COLLAR

Join shoulder seams. With RS facing and using 4mm (US 6) needles and yarn A, moss st across right front edging, K37, K49 (51: 51) across back, K37, moss st 5 from left front. 133 (135: 135) sts.
Work as folls.

Row 1 Moss st 5, P to last 5 sts, moss st to end.
Row 2 Moss st 5, K33, *sl1, K1, psso, K4, K2tog,* K41 (43: 43), rep from * to * again, K33, moss st 5.
Row 3 As row 1
Row 4 Moss st 5, K32, *sl1, K1, psso, K4, K2tog,* K39 (41: 41), rep from * to * again, K32, moss st 5.
Work dec as set on alt rows until 113 (115: 115) sts rem. Cont without shaping until collar measures 20cm (8in).
Cast off.

MAKING UP

Join side seams. Set sleeves into armhole and stitch in place. Join underarm seams. Weave in any loose ends. Press lightly using a warm iron over a damp cloth.

Tweed Cushion

SIZE & YARNS

Size	46 x 46cm
	18 x 18in

Rowan Yorkshire Tweed 4ply

A Charcoal grey (277)	6 x 25g
B Mid grey (270)	5 x 25g
C Black (283)	1 x 25g
46 x 46cm (18 x 18in) cushion pad.	

NEEDLES

1 pair of 5mm (US 8) needles.

TENSION

19 sts and 26 rows to 10cm (4in) measured over st st using 5mm (US 8) needles and double (2 ends) yarn.

CUSHION COVER

N.B. Use 2 ends of yarn throughout.
Using 5mm (US 8) needles and yarn C, cast on 91 sts. Break yarn C. Join in yarn B and knit 1 row. Change to K1, P1 rib and work 3 rows. Change to st st and cont until work meas 30cm (12in). Place markers at each end of last row. Cont in st st until work meas 46cm (18in).

Break yarn B.
Join in yarn C and work 1 row. Break yarn C.
Join in yarn A and cont in st st until work meas 76cm (30in). Place markers at each end of last row.
Cont in st st until work meas 99cm (39in), ending with WS facing for next row.
Change to K1, P1 rib and work 4 rows. Break yarn A.
Join in yarn B and purl 1 row.
Cast off.

MAKING UP

Place RS together, using markers as top and bottom of cushion cover, and overlap centre back of cushion cover by 10cm (4in). Stitch side seams. Turn RS out and press lightly using a warm iron over a damp cloth. Insert cushion pad.

Folding Cushion

SIZE & YARNS

Size	46 x 46cm
	18 x 18in

Rowan Kid Classic

A Pale grey (840)	4 x 50g
B Charcoal grey (831)	1 x 50g
46 x 46cm (18 x 18in) cushion pad.	

NEEDLES

1 pair of 5mm (US 8) needles.

TENSION

19 sts and 25 rows to 10cm (4in) measured over st st using 5mm (US 8) needles.

CUSHION COVER

Front and back (both alike)

Using 5mm (US 8) needles and yarn B, cast on 86 sts and knit 1 row. Break yarn B. Join in yarn A and, starting with a **K** row, work 71cm (28in) in st st, ending with a WS row.
Cast off.

MAKING UP

Place cast-off edges together, RS facing. Stitch side seams and cast-off edges. Turn RS out and press lightly using a warm iron over a damp cloth. Insert cushion pad. Fold over excess knitting as decorative detail.

Half-and-half Cushion

SIZE & YARNS

Size	46 x 46cm
	18 x 18in

Rowan Wool Cotton

A Black (908)	3 x 50g
B Grey (903)	2 x 50g
46 x 46cm (18 x 18in) cushion pad.	

NEEDLES

1 pair of 3.75mm (US 5) needles.

TENSION

24 sts and 32 rows to 10cm (4in) measured over st st using 3.75mm (US 5) needles.

CUSHION COVER

Using 3.75mm (US 5) needles and yarn A, cast on 111 sts. Join in yarn B and knit 1 row.
Change to K1, P1 rib and work 5 rows. Break yarn B.
Using yarn A, change to st st and cont until work meas 30cm (12in). Place markers at each end of last row.
Cont in st st until work meas 53cm (21in). Break yarn A.

Join in yarn B and cont in st st until work meas 76cm (30in). Place markers at each end of last row.
Cont in st st until work meas 99cm (39in), ending with WS facing for next row.
Join in yarn A and purl 1 row. Change to K1, P1 rib and work 5 rows. Break yarn A.
Using yarn B, purl 1 row.
Cast off.

MAKING UP

Place RS together, using markers as top and bottom of cushion cover, and overlap centre back of cushion cover by 10cm (4in). Stitch side seams. Turn RS out and press lightly using a warm iron over a damp cloth. Insert cushion pad.

LIME/LILAC

Child's Jacket
Cotton is just right for
breezy summer days.
This comfortable simple
design has garter-stitch
borders, knitted in a
softly contrasting
colour, and is ideal
for young children.
Page 100.

Fresh, clear colours, where the softness of lilac and lavender is offset by the sharp acidity of lime and lemon, are ideal for the summer months. White adds purity and calmness to the palette, and the different qualities of the yarns emphasize the texture of the knitting perfectly.

Lace Shawl
Gossamer light in a faded, soft, fluffy yarn, this delicate shawl makes the perfect cover-up for a summer's night.
Page 102.

Cable Blanket

Richly textured, this
white cable-stitch
cotton blanket has
garter-stitch borders
edged in soft lilac.
Page 103.

Garter-check Cushion

A soft double knit cotton yarn, knitted in two different garter-stitch textures, creates a great summer cushion. Page 104.

Garter-stripe Cushion

The fine quality of this garter-stitch pattern cushion in pure white with lavender details makes it perfect for the bedroom, too. Page 105.

Three-textured Cushion

Alternating colours and textures create a quirky visual impact to this, the third cushion in the group. Put all three together as here, to mix and match. Page 106.

Moss-stitch Vest

This little moss-stitch vest is trimmed with a crochet picot edge in deep lavender. The ribbon detail makes it very special, perfect for a warm summer day. Page 107.

Laundry Bag

Practical but beautiful, this laundry bag has a Victorian feel; it is knitted in fine 4ply cotton in a delicate moss-stitch diamond pattern, and trimmed with a crochet picot edge and drawstring cord in deep lavender. Page 108.

Wash Bag

Make a matching wash bag in the same yarn and stitch pattern, but in deep lavender with a citrus yellow trim and drawstring. Use it in the bathroom or take it on holiday. Page 109.

Child's Jacket

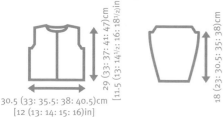

30.5 (33: 35.5: 38: 40.5)cm
[12 (13: 14: 15: 16)in]

29 (33: 37: 41: 47)cm
[11.5 (13: 14½: 16: 18½)in]

18 (23: 30.5: 35: 38)cm
[7 (9: 12: 14: 15)in]

SIZES & YARNS

	1-2	3-4	5-6	7-8	9-10	years
To fit chest	56	61	66	71	76	cm
	22	24	26	28	30	in
Actual size	61	66	71	76	81	cm
	24	26	28	30	32	in
Back length	29	33	37	41	47	cm
	11½	13	14½	16	18½	in
Sleeve seam	18	23	30.5	35	38	cm
	7	9	12	14	15	in

Rowan Handknit DK Cotton

A Lilac (305)					
4	5	5	6	7	x 50g
B Blue (287)					
1	1	1	1	1	x 50g
Buttons 5	5	5	7	7	

NEEDLES

1 pair each of 3.25mm (US 3) and 4mm (US 6) needles.

2 safety pins.

TENSION

20 sts and 28 rows to 10cm (4in) measured over st st using 4mm (US 6) needles.

BACK

Using 3.25mm (US 3) needles and yarn B, cast on 60 (65: 70: 75: 80) sts.

Knit 5 (5: 7: 7: 7) rows.

Break yarn B. Join in yarn A and change to 4mm (US 6) needles and st st.

Cont until work meas 17 (19: 21: 23: 25)cm [6½ (7½: 8½: 9: 10)in], ending with RS facing for next row.

Shape armholes

Cast off 2 (2: 3: 3: 4) sts at beg of next 2 rows.

Dec 1 st at each end of next and foll alt rows until 52 (55: 58: 61: 64) sts rem. Cont without shaping until work meas 28 (32: 36: 40: 46)cm [11 (12½: 14: 15½: 18)in], ending with RS facing for next row.

Shape shoulders

Sizes 1 and 2

Cast off 16 (17) sts at beg of next 2 rows.

Cast off.

Sizes 3, 4 and 5

Cast off 6 (6: 7) sts at beg of next 4 rows.

Cast off 6 (7: 6) sts at beg of next 2 rows.

Cast off.

LEFT FRONT

Using 3.25mm (US 3) needles and yarn B, cast on 34 (36: 38: 41: 43) sts.

Knit 5 (5: 7: 7: 7) rows.

Break yarn B. Join in yarn A and change to 4mm (US 6) needles and st st.

Row 1 K30 (32: 34: 37: 39), leave last 4 sts on safety pin.

Cont in st st until work measures 17 (19: 21: 23: 25)cm [6½ (7½: 8½: 9: 10)in], ending with RS facing for next row.

Shape armhole

Cast off 2 (2: 3: 3: 4) sts, K to end.

Purl 1 row.

Dec 1 st at beg of next and foll alt rows until 26 (27: 28: 30: 31) sts rem.

Cont without shaping until work is 11 (11: 7: 7: 9) rows LESS than back at shoulder, ending with **WS** facing for next row.

Shape neck

Sizes 1 and 2

Row 1 WS facing, cast off 5 sts, work to end.

Rows 2 to 5 Dec 1 st at neck edge.

Row 6 K to end.

Row 7 Dec 1 st at neck edge.

Rows 8 to 11 St st.

Cast off.

Sizes 3, 4 and 5

Row 1 Cast off 5 (6: 6) sts, work to end.

Rows 2 to 5 Dec 1 st at neck edge.

Row 6 K to end.

Row 7 Dec 1 st at neck edge.

Size 5 ONLY work 2 rows in st st.

Shape shoulder

Cast off 6 (6: 7) sts at beg of next and foll
all row.

Work 1 row. Cast off rem 6 (7: 6) sts.

RIGHT FRONT

Work as for left front, reversing all shaping
and starting neck 10 (10: 6: 6: 8) rows LESS
than back at shoulder.

SLEEVES (make 2)

Using 3.25mm (US 3) needles and yarn B, cast
on 33 (35: 37: 40: 42) sts and knit 5 (5: 7: 7: 7)
rows. Break yarn B. Join in yarn A and change
to 4mm (US 6) needles and st st.

Inc 1 st at each end of 5th and every foll 4th

(4th: 5th: 6th 6th) row to 53 (55: 59: 60:
64) sts.

Cont without shaping until work meas 18 (23:
30.5: 35: 38)cm [7 (9: 12: 14: 15)in], ending
with RS facing for next row.

Shape sleevehead

Cast off 2 (2: 3: 3: 4) sts at beg of next 2 rows.
Dec 1 st at each end of next and foll alt rows
until 45 (45: 47: 46: 48) sts rem. Cast off
loosely.

BUTTON BAND

Using 3.25mm (US 3) needles and yarn A and
with RS of left front facing, pick up loop before
4 sts on safety pin and K into back of it, K
across 4 sts on safety pin. Work in K1, P1 rib
until band, when slightly stretched, fits to neck
of left front. Cast off. Sew band to left front.
Mark positions for buttons, the first 1cm (½in)
from neck, the remainder at regular intervals,
ending before the garter-stitch hem.

BUTTONHOLE BAND

Work as for button band, rejoining yarn with
WS facing and purling across row. Make
buttonholes by rib 1, K2tog, yon, rib 2, to

correspond with marked button positions. Sew
band to right front.

COLLAR

Using 3.25mm (US 3) needles and yarn A, cast
on 55 (57: 61: 65: 71) sts and work in g st for
5.5 (5.5: 6: 6.5: 7)cm [2 (2: 2½: 2½: 2¾)in].
Cast off.

MAKING UP

Join shoulder and side seams. Join sleeve
seams. Starting and finishing halfway across
front bands, pin cast-off edge of collar around
neck, RS of collar to WS of garment. Sew into
place. Weave in any loose ends. Pin sleeves to
body, centre of sleeve top to shoulder seam,
and stitch into place. Sew on buttons. Press
lightly using a warm iron over a damp cloth.

Lace Shawl

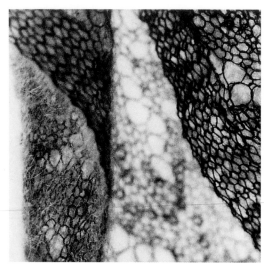

SIZE & YARNS

Size	124 x 124cm
	49 x 49in

Rowan Kidsilk Haze

A Grape (600)	9 x 25g
B Green (597)	Small amount for edging.

NEEDLES

1 pair each of 4mm (US 6) and 5mm (US 8) needles.

TENSION

23 sts to 10cm (4in) wide measured over pattern using 4mm (US 6) needles after pressing.

SHAWL

Using 5mm (US 8) needles and yarn B, cast on 285 sts. Break yarn B. Join in yarn A and change to 4mm (US 6) needles and work lace patt as folls.

Row 1 K6, *K2, sl1, K1, psso, K4, K2tog, K2, yon, K1, yon, rep from * to last 6 sts, K6.

Row 2 and alt rows K6, P to last 6 sts, K6.

Row 3 K6, *yon, K2, sl1, K1, psso, K2, K2tog, K2, yon, K3, rep from * to last 6 sts, K6.

Row 5 K6, *K1, yon, K2, sl1, K1, psso, K2tog, K2, yon, K4, rep from * rep to last 6 sts, K6.

Row 7 K6, *yon, K1, yon, K2, sl1, K1, psso, K4, K2tog, K2, rep from * to last 6 sts, K6.

Row 9 K6, *K3, yon, K2, sl1, K1, psso, K2, K2tog, K2, yon, rep from * to last 6 sts, K6.

Row 11 K6, *K4, yon, K2, sl1, K1, psso, K2tog, K2, yon, K1, rep from * to last 6 sts, K6.

Row 12 As row 2.

Rows 1 to 12 form lace patt.

Rep rows 1 to 12 until work meas 124cm (49in), ending with WS row facing for next row. Break yarn A.

Join in yarn B and purl 1 row.

Change to 5mm (US 8) needles and cast off loosely.

MAKING UP

Weave in any loose ends. Press lightly using a warm iron over a damp cloth.

Cable Blanket

SIZE & YARNS

Size	84 x 122cm
	33 x 48in

Rowan Handknit DK Cotton

A White (263)	14 x 50g
B Lilac (305)	1 x 50g

NEEDLES

1 pair of 4.5mm (US 7) needles.
Cable needle.

TENSION

19 sts and 26 rows to 10cm (4in) measured over st st using 4.5mm (US 7) needles.

SPECIAL ABBREVIATIONS

c4b = place next 2 sts on cable needle, leave at back of work, K2, K2 from cable needle.

THROW

Using 4.5mm (US 7) needles and yarn B, cast on 159 sts. Break yarn B. Join in yarn A and knit 8 rows.
Change to cable patt as folls.
Row 1 K5, *P1, K4, P1, K5, rep from * to end.

Row 2 K6, *P4, K1, P5, K1, rep from * to last 10 sts, P4, K6.
Row 3 K5, *P1, c4b, P1, K5, rep from * to end.
Row 4 As row 2.
Row 5 K5, *P1, K4, P6; rep from ^ to last 11 sts, P1, K4, P1, K5.
Row 6 As row 2.
Rows 1 to 6 form cable patt with g st edge.
Rep rows 1 to 6 until work meas 120cm (47in), ending with RS facing for next row. Knit 9 rows. Break yarn A.
Join in yarn B and purl 1 row.
Cast off.

MAKING UP

Weave in any loose ends. Press lightly using a warm iron over a damp cloth.

Garter-check Cushion

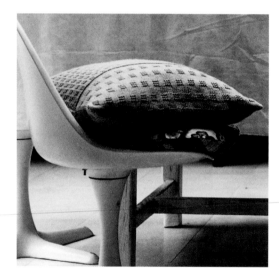

SIZE & YARNS

Size	46 x 46cm
	18 x 18in

Rowan Handknit DK Cotton

A Lilac (305)	6 x 50g
B Green (219)	1 x 50g

46 x 46cm (18 x 18in) cushion pad.

NEEDLES

1 pair each of 3.75mm (US 5) and 4mm (US 6) needles.

TENSION

20 sts and 28 rows to 10cm (4in) measured over st st using 4mm (US 6) needles.

CUSHION COVER

Using 3.75mm (US 5) needles and yarn A, cast on 92 sts. Join in yarn B and work 6 rows in K1, P1 rib. Break yarn B.
Change to 4mm (US 6) needles, yarn A and st st. Work patt 1 as folls.
Rows 1 to 6 St st.
Row 7 K1, *K3, P3, rep from * to last st, K1.
Row 8 P to end.

Rows 9 to 12 As rows 7 and 8, twice.
Rows 13 to 18 St st.
Row 19 K1, *P3, K3, rep from * to last st, K1.
Row 20 P to end.
Rows 21 to 24 As rows 19 and 20, twice.
Rows 1 to 24 form patt rep. Work 4 more repeats, then rows 1 to 18 again. 138 rows in patt 1.
Join in yarn B and knit 2 rows. Break yarn B. Using yarn A, work patt 2 as folls.
Rows 1 and 2 St st.
Row 3 K2, *P2, K4, rep from * to end.
Row 4 P to end.
Rows 5 and 6 As rows 3 and 4.
Row 7 K1, *K4, P2, rep from * to last st, K1.
Row 8 P to end.
Rows 9 and 10 As rows 7 and 8.
Rows 3 to 10 form patt rep. Rep rows 3 to 10 until work measures approx 98cm (38½in), ending with row 6 or 10.
Next row K to end.
Join in yarn B, change to 3.75mm (US 5) needles and purl 1 row.
Work 6 rows in K1, P1 rib.
Break yarn B.
Using yarn A, cast off in rib.

MAKING UP

Measure 30cm (11¾in) from cast-on edge, place pins to mark first fold. Measure a further 46cm (18in) and place pins to mark 2nd fold. Placing RS together, make first fold, then 2nd fold, overlapping at centre back of cushion cover by 10cm (4in). Stitch side seams. Turn RS out and press lightly using a warm iron over a damp cloth. Insert cushion pad.

Garter-stripe Cushion

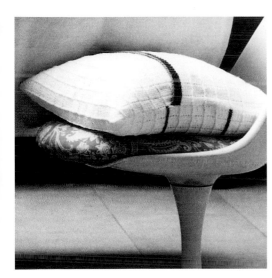

SIZE & YARNS

Size	46 x 46cm
	18 x 18in

Rowan Cotton Glace

A White (726)	6 x 50g
B Lavender (787)	1 x 50g
C Green (814)	Small amount.
46 x 46cm (18 x 18in) cushion pad.	

NEEDLES

1 pair each of 3.25mm (US 3) and 3.75mm
(US 5) needles.

TENSION

23 sts and 32 rows to 10cm (4in) measured
over st st using 3.75mm (US 5) needles.

CUSHION COVER

Using 3.25mm (US 3) needles and yarn C, cast
on 104 sts. Break yarn C. Join in yarn B and
work 6 rows in K1, P1 rib. Break yarn B.
Change to 3.75mm (US 5) needles and join in
yarn A. Work in patt as folls.
Row 1 K to end.
Row 2 *P6, K1, rep from * to last 6 sts, P6.

Rows 3 to 8 As rows 1 and 2, three times.
Rows 9 and 10 K to end.
Rows 1 to 10 form patt rep. Cont in patt until
work meas 30cm (12in). Place markers at each
end of last row. Cont until work meas approx
46cm (18in), ending with row 8. Join in yarn B.
Knit 2 rows. Break yarn B.
Using yarn A, work rows 1 to 10 four times,
then rows 1 to 8 again. Join in yarn C and knit
2 rows. Break yarn C.
Using yarn A, cont in patt until work meas
76cm (30in). Place markers at each end of
last row.
Cont until work meas approx 99cm (39in),
ending with row 8. Break yarn A.
Change to 3.25mm (US 3) needles and join in
yarn B. Knit 1 row. Work 5 rows in K1, P1 rib.
Break yarn B. Join in yarn C and cast off in rib.

MAKING UP

Place RS together, using markers as top and
bottom of cushion cover, and overlap centre
back of cushion cover by 10cm (4in). Stitch
side seams. Turn RS out and press lightly
using a warm iron over a damp cloth.
Insert cushion pad.

Three-textured Cushion

SIZE & YARNS

| Size | 46 x 46cm |
| | 18 x 18in |

Rowan Cotton Glace

A Pale lime (813)	3 x 50g
B Lavender (787)	1 x 50g
C Lilac (811)	1 x 50g
D Green (814)	3 x 50g

46 x 46cm (18 x 18in) cushion pad.

NEEDLES

1 pair each of 3.25 (US 3) and 3.75mm (US 5) needles.

TENSION

23 sts and 32 rows to 10cm (4in) measured over st st using 3.75mm (US 5) needles.

CUSHION COVER

Using 3.25mm (US 3) needles and yarn A, cast on 104 sts.

Join in yarn B and work 7 rows in K1, P1 rib. Break yarn B.

Change to 3.75mm (US 5) needles and yarn A. Purl 1 row.

Work in patt as folls.

Row 1 K2, *K5, (P1, K1) twice, P1, rep from * to last 2 sts, K2.

Row 2 K2, P1, *K1, P1, K1, P7, rep from * to last st, K1.

Rows 3 to 8 As rows 1 and 2, three times.

Row 9 K2, *(P1, K1) twice, P1, K5, rep from * to last 2 sts, K2.

Row 10 K1, *P7, K1, P1, K1, rep from * to last 3 sts, P2, K1.

Rows 11 to 16 As rows 9 and 10, three times.

Rows 1 to 16 form patt rep. Cont in patt until work meas 30cm (12in). Place markers at each end of last row. Cont in patt until work meas approx 46cm (18in), ending with row 8 or 16. Break yarn A.

Join in yarn B and knit 2 rows. Break yarn B. Join in yarn C and knit 1 row.

Change to moss stitch and cont until work meas 61cm (24in), ending with RS facing for next row. Break yarn C.

Join in yarn B and knit 2 rows. Break yarn B. Join in yarn D and knit 1 row.

Change to patt as folls.

Row 1 K1, *P7, K1, P1, K1, rep from * to last 3 sts, P2, K1.

Row 2 K2, *(P1, K1) twice, P1, K5, rep from * to last 2 sts, K2.

Rows 1 and 2 form patt rep. Cont in patt until work measures 76cm (30in). Place markers at each end of last row. Cont until work meas approx 99cm (39in), ending with row 1. Break yarn D.

Change to 3.25mm (US 3) needles, join in yarn B and knit 1 row. Work 6 rows in K1, P1 rib. Break yarn B. Join in yarn A and cast off in rib.

MAKING UP

Place RS together, using markers as top and bottom of cushion cover, and overlap centre back of cushion cover by 10cm (4in). Stitch side seams. Turn RS out and press lightly using a warm iron over a damp cloth. Insert cushion pad.

Moss-stitch Vest

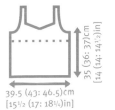

39.5 (43: 46.5)cm
[15½ (17: 18¼)in]

35 (36: 37)cm
[14 (14: 14½)in]

SIZES & YARNS

Size	S	M	L	
To fit bust	76-81	86	91	cm
	30-32	34	36	in
Actual size	79	86	93	cm
	31	34	36½	in
Centre back length	35	36	37	cm
	14	14	14½	in

Rowan Cotton Glace

A Pale lime (813)	6	6	7	x 50g
B Lavender (787)	1	1	1	x 50g

1.8m (2yd) narrow maroon ribbon

NEEDLES

1 pair each of 2.75mm (US 2) and 3.25mm
(US 3) needles.

3mm (US D3) crochet hook.

TENSION

24 sts and 34 rows to 10cm (4in) measured
over st st using 3.25mm (US 3) needles.

BACK

Using 2.75mm (US 2) needles and yarn A, cast
on 95 (103: 111) sts.

Work 6 rows in K1, P1 rib.

Change to 3.25mm (US 3) needles and work in
rib as folls.

Row 1 *K3, P1, rep from * to last 3 sts, K3.

Row 2 *P3, K1, rep from * to last 3 sts, P3.

Rep rows 1 and 2 until work meas 21cm (8½in),
ending with row 1.

Make eyelets

Next row (WS) *P2tog, yon, P1, K1, rep from *
to last 3 sts, P2tog, yon, P1.

Work 2 more rows in rib.

Change to moss st and cont until work meas
33cm (13in).

Shape armholes

Rows 1 and 2 Cast off 5 (6: 7) sts at beg of row.

Dec 1 st at each end of next 6 (8: 10) rows. 73
(75: 77) sts.

Divide for neck

Next row Moss st 36 (37: 38), cast off 1 st,
moss st to end. 36 (37: 38) sts.

Row 1 Dec 1 st at each end of row.

Row 2 Dec 1 st at neck edge.

Rep rows 1 and 2 until 6 (5: 5) sts rem. Size 1
only, dec 1 st at neck edge on next row.

Cont on these 5 sts until moss st section of
work meas 28cm (11in). Cast off.

With WS facing, rejoin yarn to rem sts at centre
and work to match first side, reversing shaping.

FRONT

Make a second piece to match.

TRIMS

Join shoulder seams.

With RS facing and using 3mm (US D3) crochet
hook and yarn B, work an edging of double
crochet (US single crochet) and picots around
armholes and neck as folls.

Picot edging *Work 3dc along edge, then work
3ch and join with a slip st to last dc to make
picot, rep from *.

MAKING UP

Join side seams. Weave in any loose ends.
Press lightly using a warm iron over a damp
cloth. Weave ribbon through eyelets and
tie at front.

Laundry Bag

SIZE & YARNS

Size	51.5 x 61cm
	20 x 24in

Rowan 4ply Cotton

A White (113)	7 x 50g
B Deep lavender (127)	1 x 50g

NEEDLES

1 pair of 3mm (US 2/3) needles.
3mm (US D3) crochet hook.

TENSION

28 sts and 38 rows to 10cm (4in) measured over pattern using 3mm (US 2/3) needles.

BAG

Using 3mm (US 2/3) needles and yarn A, cast on 144 sts and work 6cm (2½in) in st st.

Make eyelets

Row 1 K4, *cast off 1 st, K6, rep from * to last 4 sts, cast off 1 st, K2.

Row 2 *P3, yon, P4, rep from * to end.

Work 2 rows in st st.

Change to diamond patt as folls.

Row 1 *P1, K7, rep from * to end.

Row 2 *K1, P5, K1, P1, rep from * to end.

Row 3 *K2, P1, K3, P1, K1, rep from * to end.

Row 4 *P2, K1, P1, K1, P3, rep from * to end.

Row 5 *K4, P1, K3, rep from * to end.

Row 6 As row 4.

Row 7 As row 3.

Row 8 As row 2.

Rows 1 to 8 form diamond patt rep.

Rep rows 1 to 8 until work meas approx 61cm (24in), ending with a WS row.

Cast off.

Make second piece to match.

MAKING UP

Weave in any loose ends. Place RS together, taking care to match diamonds and eyelets, and stitch side and bottom seams.

Using 3mm (US D3) crochet hook and yarn B, work a picot edging around top opening of bag as folls.

Work a round of double crochet (US single crochet) around top.

Next round *1dc in each of next 3dc, then work 3ch and join with a slip st to last dc to make picot, rep from * to end.

Make 2 drawstring ties by using 3 ends of yarn B and working a crochet chain for 127cm (50in), leaving 7cm (3in) lengths at each end for tassels. Thread through eyelets, one each way (see photograph), and pull to close bag. Press lightly using a warm iron over a damp cloth.

Wash Bag

SIZE & YARNS

Size	25 x 33cm
	10 x 13in

Rowan 4ply Cotton

A Deep lavender (127)	2 x 50g
B Pale lime (134)	1 x 50g

NEEDLES

1 pair of 3mm (US 2/3) needles.
3mm (US D3) crochet hook.

TENSION

28 sts and 38 rows to 10cm (4in) measured over pattern using 3mm (US 2/3) needles.

BAG

Using 3mm (US 2/3) needles and yarn A, cast on 72 sts and work 5cm (2in) in st st.

Make eyelets

Row 1 K4, *cast off 1 st, K6, rep from * to last 4 sts, cast off 1 st, K2.

Row 2 *P3, yon, P4, rep from * to end.

Work 2 rows in st st.

Change to diamond patt as folls.

Row 1 *P1, K7, rep from * to end.

Row 2 *K1, P5, K1, P1, rep from * to end.

Row 3 *K2, P1, K3, P1, K1, rep from * to end.

Row 4 *P2, K1, P1, K1, P3, rep from * to end.

Row 5 *K4, P1, K3, rep from * to end.

Row 6 As row 4.

Row 7 As row 3.

Row 8 As row 2.

Rows 1 to 8 form diamond patt rep.

Rep rows 1 to 8 until work meas approx 33cm (13in), ending with a WS row.

Cast off.

Make second piece to match.

MAKING UP

Weave in any loose ends. Place RS together, taking care to match diamonds and eyelets, and stitch side and bottom seams.

Using 3mm (US D3) crochet hook and yarn B, work a picot edging around top opening of bag as folls.

Work a round of double crochet (US single crochet) around top.

Next round *1dc in each of next 3dc, then work 3ch and join with a slip st to last dc to make picot, rep from * to end.

Make 2 drawstring ties by using 3 ends of yarn B and working a crochet chain for 76cm (30in), leaving 7cm (3in) lengths at each end for tassels. Thread through eyelets, one each way (see photograph), and pull to close bag.

Press lightly using a warm iron over a damp cloth.

USEFUL INFORMATION

Knitting Techniques

Included here is information that will help you follow knitting patterns and achieve success with your knits. (See page 117 for knitting abbreviations.)

TENSION

Obtaining the correct tension (the correct number of stitches and rows per cm/in) is perhaps the single factor that can make the difference between a successful piece of knitting and a disastrous one. It is especially important for knitted garments. Tension controls both the shape and size of an article, so any variation, however slight, can distort the finished garment. It is recommended that you knit a square in the pattern stitch and/or stocking stitch (depending on the pattern instructions) of perhaps 5 to 10 more stitches and 5 to 10 more rows than those given in the tension note. Mark the central 10cm (4in) square with pins and count the number or rows and stitches within this area. If you have more stitches and rows than the recommended tension, try again using thicker needles; if you have fewer stitches and rows, try again using finer needles. Once you have achieved the correct tension, your garment will be knit to precisely the measurements indicated.

SIZES

In a pattern that is written for more than one size, the first figure in the set of figures for different sizes is for the smallest size and the figures for the larger sizes are inside the parentheses. When there is only one set of figures, this applies to all sizes. Be sure to follow the set of figures for your chosen size throughout.

When choosing which size to knit, look first at the actual measurement around the garment at the underarm point – this is given under the size list at the beginning of the pattern. A useful tip is to measure one of your own garments that fits you comfortably. Having chosen an appropriate pattern size based on width, look at the corresponding length for that size; if you are not happy with the recommended length, adjust your own garment before beginning your armhole shaping – any adjustment after this point will mean that the sleeve will not fit into your garment easily. Don't forget to take your adjustment into account if there is any side seam shaping.

Finally, look at the sleeve length, taking into account any top-arm insertion length. Measure your body between the centre of your neck and your wrist; this measurement should correspond to half the garment width plus the sleeve length. Again, your sleeve length may be adjusted, but remember to take into consideration your sleeve increases if you do adjust the length – you must increase more frequently than the pattern states to shorten your sleeve, less frequently to lengthen it.

KNITTING WITH COLOUR

There are two main methods of working colour into a knitted fabric – the intarsia and Fair Isle techniques. The first method produces a single thickness of fabric and is usually used where a colour is only required in a particular area of a row and does not form a repeating pattern across the row, as in the Fair Isle technique.

INTARSIA

The simplest way to work the intarsia technique is to cut short lengths of yarn for each motif or block of colour used in a row. Then when joining in the various colours at the appropriate point on the row, link one colour to the next by twisting them around each other where they meet on the wrong side to avoid gaps. All loose ends can either be darned in later along the colour join lines, or can be woven into the back of the knitting as each colour is used. Weaving in the ends while knitting is done in much the same way as weaving in yarns when working the Fair Isle technique and does save time darning-in ends later. It is essential that the tension is noted for intarsia as this may vary from the stocking stitch if both are used in the same pattern.

FAIR ISLE TYPE KNITTING

When two or three colours are worked repeatedly across a row, strand the yarn not in use loosely across the wrong side of the knitting. If you are working with more than two colours, treat the floating yarns as if they were one yarn and always spread the stitches to their correct width to keep them elastic. It is advisable not to carry the stranded or floating yarns over more than three stitches at a time, but to weave them under and over the colour you are working, catching them into the back of the work.

FINISHING INSTRUCTIONS

The pieces for your knitted garment or other projects may take hours to complete, so it would be a great pity to spoil the work by taking too little care in the pressing and finishing process. Follow the following these tips for professional-looking knits.

PRESSING AND BLOCKING

Spread out each piece of knitting to the correct measurements and pin it to a backing cloth – this is called 'blocking'. Following the instructions on the yarn label, press the pieces, avoiding ribbing, garter-stitch areas and other raised textures such as cables. Take special care to press the edges, as this will make stitching seams both easier and neater. If the yarn label indicates that the fabric is not to be pressed, then cover the blocked out knitted fabric with a damp white cotton cloth and leave it to stand to create the desired effect.

Darn in all ends neatly along the selvedge edge or a colour join, as appropriate.

STITCHING SEAMS

When stitching knitted pieces together, remember to match areas of colour and texture very carefully where they meet. Use a seam stitch such as backstitch or mattress stitch (an edge-to-edge stitch) for all main knitting seams. Join all ribbing (and neckbands) with mattress stitch, unless otherwise stated.

JOINING GARMENT PIECES

When stitching the seams on a knitted garment, start by joining the left shoulder and neckband seams as explained above. Then sew the top of the sleeve to the body of the garment using the method recommended in the pattern. The following are the techniques for different sleeve types.

Straight cast-off sleeves: Aligning the centre of the cast-off edge of the sleeve with the shoulder seam, sew the top of the sleeve to the body, using markers as guidelines where applicable.

Square set-in sleeves: Aligning the centre of the cast-off edge of the sleeve with the shoulder seam, set the sleevehead into the armhole so that the straight sides at the top of the sleeve form a neat right-angle with the armhole cast-off stitches on the back and front.

Shallow set-in sleeves: Aligning the centre of cast-off edge of sleeve with the shoulder seam, join the cast-off stitches at the beginning of the armhole shaping with the cast-off stitches at the start of the sleevehead shaping. Sew the sleevehead into the armhole, easing in the shapings.

Set-in sleeves: Aligning the centre of the cast-off edge of sleeve with the shoulder seam, set in the sleeve, easing the sleevehead into the armhole.

After joining the top of the sleeves to the back and front of the garment, join the side and sleeve seams.

Next, slip stitch any pocket edgings and linings in place, and sew on buttons to correspond with buttonholes.

Lastly, press seams, avoiding ribbing and any areas of garter stitch.

Knitting Abbreviations

ABBREVIATIONS

The following abbreviations are used for the patterns in this book. Explanations for special abbreviations are given with the patterns.

alt	alternate
approx	approximately
beg	begin(ning)
cm	centimetre(s)
cont	continu(e)(ing)
dec	decreas(e)(ing)
foll(s)	follow(s)(ing)
g st	garter stitch (K every row)
in	inch(es)
inc	increas(e)(ing); in a row instruction work into front and back of stitch
K	knit
m	metre(s)
M1	make one stitch by picking up horizontal loop before next stitch and knitting into back of it

M1P	make one stitch by picking up horizontal loop before next stitch and purling into back of it
meas	measures
mm	millimetre(s)
moss st	work in moss stitch (see right)
oz	ounce(s)
P	purl
patt	pattern
psso	pass slipped stitch over
p2sso	pass 2 slipped stitches over
rem	remain(s)(ing)
rep	repeat(ing)
rev st st	reverse stocking stitch (P all RS rows, K all WS rows)
RS	right side(s)
sl1	slip one stitch
st(s)	stitch(es)
st st	stocking stitch (K all RS rows, P all WS rows)
tbl	through back of loop(s)
tog	together

WS	wrong side(s)
yb	yarn to back of work between two needles
yd	yard(s)
yf	yarn to front of work between two needles
yon	yarn over right-hand needle to make a new stitch
o (zero)	no stitches, times or rows for that size

MOSS STITCH

Where a pattern calls for 'moss st', work over an 'even number of stitches' as folls.

Moss st row 1 (K1, P1) to end.
Moss st row 2 (P1, K1) to end.
Rep rows 1 and 2 for patt.
Work over an 'odd number of stitches' as folls.
Moss st row 1 *K1, P1, rep from * to last st, K1.
Rep row 1 for patt.

Yarn Information

The following list covers the Rowan yarns used in this book. All the information was correct at the time of publication, but yarn companies change their products frequently and cannot absolutely guarantee that the shades or yarn types used will be available when you come to use these patterns. The yarn descriptions here will help you find a substitute if necessary. If substituting yarn, always remember to calculate the yarn amount needed by metrage/yardage rather than by ball weight.

Note: Always check the yarn label for care instructions.

Rowan Cotton Glace

A medium-weight cotton yarn; 100 per cent cotton
Ball size 50g/1¾oz ball; about 115m (126yd)
Recommended tension 23 sts and 32 rows to 10cm (4in) measured over st st using 3.25–3.75mm (US sizes 3–5) needles

Rowan 4ply Cotton

A lightweight cotton yarn; 100 per cent cotton
Ball size 50g/1¾oz; about 170m (186yd)

Recommended tension 27–29 sts and 37–39 rows to 10cm (4in) measured over st st using 3–3.25mm (US sizes 2–3) needles

Rowan 4ply Soft

A lightweight wool yarn; 100 per cent merino wool
Ball size 50g/1¾oz; about 175m (191yd)
Recommended tension 28 sts and 36 rows to 10cm (4in) measured over st st using 3.25mm (US size 3) needles

Rowan Handknit DK Cotton

A medium-weight cotton yarn; 100 per cent cotton
Ball size 50g/1¾oz; about 85m (93yd)
Recommended tension 19–20 sts and 28 rows to 10cm (4in) measured over st st using 4–4.5mm (US sizes 6–7) needles

Rowan Kid Classic

A medium-weight mohair-mix yarn; 70 per cent lambswool, 26 per cent kid mohair, 4 per cent nylon
Ball size 50g/1¾oz; about 140m (153yd)
Recommended tension 18–19 sts and 23–25

rows to 10cm (4in) measured over st st using 5–5.5mm (US sizes 8–9) needles

Rowan Kidsilk Haze

A lightweight mohair-mix yarn; 70 per cent super kid mohair, 30 per cent silk
Ball size 25g/1oz; about 210m (229yd)
Recommended tension 18–25 sts and 23–34 rows to 10cm (4in) measured over st st using 3.25–5mm (US sizes 3–8) needles

Rowan Polar

A chunky wool-mix yarn; 60 per cent pure new wool, 30 per cent alpaca, 10 per cent acrylic
Ball size 100g/3½oz; about 100m (109yd)
Recommended tension 12 sts and 16 rows to 10cm (4in) measured over st st using 8mm (US size 11) needles

Rowan Summer Tweed

A medium-weight silk/cotton blend yarn; 70 per cent silk, 30 per cent cotton
Hank size 50g/1¾oz; about 108m (118yd)
Recommended tension 16 sts and 23 rows to 10cm (4in) measured over st st using 5mm (US size 8) needles

Rowan Wool Cotton

A medium-weight wool/cotton blend yarn; 50 per cent merino wool, 50 per cent cotton
Ball size 50g/1¾oz; about 113m (123yd)
Recommended tension 22–24 sts and 30–32 rows to 10cm (4in) measured over st st using 3.75–4mm (US sizes 5–6) needles

Rowan Yorkshire Tweed DK

A medium-weight wool yarn; 100 per cent pure new wool
Ball size 50g/1¾oz; about 113m (123yd)
Recommended tension 20–22 sts and 28–30 rows to 10cm (4in) measured over st st using 4mm (US size 6) needles

Rowan Yorkshire Tweed 4ply

A lightweight wool yarn; 100 per cent pure new wool
Ball size 25g/1oz; about 110m (120yd)
Recommended tension 26–28 sts and 38–40 rows to 10cm (4in) measured over st st using 3–3.25mm (US sizes 2–3) needles

Buying Yarn

For the best results, always use the yarn specified in your knitting pattern. See the Rowan addresses below to find a stockist near you. For all other countries, contact the main office in the U.K.

ROWAN YARN ADDRESSES

U.K. Rowan, Green Lane Mill, Holmfirth, West Yorkshire HD9 2DX, England.
Tel: +44 (0) 1484 681 881. Fax: +44 (0) 1484 687 920. **www.knitrowan.com**

Australia Australian Country Spinners, 314 Albert Street, Brunswick, Victoria 3056.
Tel: (03) 9380 3888.

Belgium Pavan, Meerlaanstraat 73, B9860 Balegem (Oosterzele). Tel: (32) 9 221 8594.
E-mail: pavan@pandora.be

Canada Diamond Yarn, 9697 St Laurent, Montreal, Quebec, H3L 2N1. Tel: (514) 388 6188.
Diamond Yarn (Toronto), 155 Martin Ross, Unit 3, Toronto, Ontario M3J 2L9. Tel: (416) 736 6111.
www.diamondyarns.com
E-mail: diamond@diamondyarn.com

Denmark Designvaerkstedet, Boulevarden 9, Aalborg 9000. Tel: (45) 9812 0713. Fax: (45) 9813 0213.
Inger's, Volden 19, Aarhus 8000.
Tel: (45) 8619 4044.
Sommerfuglen, Vandkunsten 3, Kobenhaven K 1467. Tel: (45) 3332 8290.
E-mail: mail@sommerfuglen.dk
www.sommerfuglen.dk
Uldstedet, Fiolstraede 13, Kobehavn K 1171.
Tel/Fax: (45) 3391 1771.
Uldstedet, G1. Jernbanevej 7, Lyngby 2800.
Tel/Fax: (45) 4588 1088.
Garnhoekeren, Karen Olsdatterstraede 9, Ruskilde 4000. Tel/Fax: (45) 4637 2063.

France Elle Tricot, 8 Rue du Coq, 67000 Strasbourg. Tel: (33) 3 88 23 03 13.
E-mail: elletricot@agat.net
elletricot@agat.net. www.elletricote.com

Germany Wolle & Design, Wolfshovener Strasse 76, 52428 Julich-Stetternich.
Tel: (49) 2461 54735.
www.wolleunddesign.de
E-mail: Info@wolleunddesign.de

Holland de Afstap, Oude Leliestraat 12, 1015 AW Amsterdam. Tel: (31) 20 6231445.

Hong Kong East Unity Co Ltd, Unit B2, 7/F Block B, Kailey Industrial Centre, 12 Fung Yip Street, Chai Wan. Tel: (852) 2869 7110.
Fax (852) 2537 6952.
E-mail: eastuni@netvigator.com

Iceland Storkurinn, Laugavegi 59, 101 Reykjavik. Tel: (354) 551 8258. Fax: (354) 562 8252. E-mail: malin@mmedia.is

Japan Puppy Co Ltd, T151-0051, 3-16-5 Sendagaya, Shibuyaku, Tokyo. Tel: (81) 3 3490 2827. E-mail: info@rowan-jaeger.com

Korea De Win Co Ltd, Chongam Bldg, 101, 34-7 Samsung-dong, Seoul. Tel: (82) 2 511 1087.
E-mail: knittking@yahoo.co.kr www.dewin.co.kr
My Knit Studio, (3F) 121 Kwan Hoon Dong, Chongro-ku, Seoul. Tel: (82) 2 722 0006.
E-mail: myknit@myknit.com

New Zealand Alterknitives, PO Box 47961, Ponsonby, Auckland. Tel: (64) 9 376 0337.

E-mail: knitit@ihug.co.nz
Knit World, PO Box 30 645, Lower Hutt. Tel: (64) 4 586 4530. E-mail: knitting@xtra.co.nz
The Stitchery, Shop 8, Suncourt Shopping Centre, 1111 Taupo. Tel: (64) 7 378 9195.

Norway Paa Pinne, Tennisvn 3D, 0777 Oslo.
Tel: (47) 909 62 818. www.paapinne.no
E-mail: design@paapinne.no

Spain Oyambre, Pau Claris 145, 80009 Barcelona. Tel: (34) 670 011957.
E-mail: comercial@oyambreonline.com

Sweden Wincent, Norrtullsgatan 65, 113 45 Stockholm. Tel: (46) 8 33 70 60.
E-mail: wincent@chello.se www.wincent.nu

U.S.A. Rowan USA, c/o Westminster Fibers Inc, 4 Townsend West, Suite 8, Nashua, NH 03063.
Tel: +1 (603) 886 5041/5043.
E-mail: rowan@westminsterfibers.com

Acknowledgments

Author's Acknowledgments

My warmest thanks to all the people who have contributed to this book for their enthusiasm, encouragement, and commitment.

Stephen Sheard, Kate Buller, Ann Hinchcliffe and Sarah Hatton at Rowan; Eva Yates, Gill Everett and her team of knitters; Stella Smith; Sally Harding, Hilary Laurence, and Elizabeth Dallas; Chloe, Josie, Hannah and Alicia; Catherine Gratwicke, Francine Kay and Alesse Bowditch, Georgina Rhodes, and Susan Berry.

To my family for their constant support and endless patience.

And especially to Georgina Dallas, who inspired the idea for the book.

Publisher's Acknowledgments

The publishers would like to thank everyone on the team who helped to put this book together, in particular Georgina Rhodes and Richard Proctor, Catherine Gratwicke, Francine Kay, Eva Yates, Stella Smith, and Sally Harding.